Spelling Success

CLASS 3

Peter Clutterbuck

Blake
EDUCATION
Better ways to learn

To Jessie O'Brien

Spelling Success Class 3

Published by Scholastic India Pvt. Ltd.
A-27, Ground Floor, Sigma Centre
Infocity-1, Sector 34, Gurgaon-122001 (India)
Info-in@scholastic.asia

Author: Peter Clutterbuck
Editor: Kerry Davies
Cover and internal design: Janice Bowles
Typesetter: Julian Mole, Post Pre Press.

ISBN: 978-93-5471-960-8
First edition 2010
This reprint edition: June 2024
Printed in India

Contents

Term 1

✓ Tick when completed

Term 2

✓ Tick when completed

Contents continued

About This Book

The *Spelling Success* series provides students with learning activities that embrace the different elements of the spelling system. Each book focuses on the different scope and sequences in the development of spelling skills for each age group or skill level.

These books are not a complete spelling course in themselves, neither are they meant to be, but they provide both students and teachers with the content needed to produce best practices in spelling.

The activities in each book are sequential through the four terms of the school year. This means that it's best to start at the beginning of the Term 1 section and work though to the end, before commencing Term 2 activities, and so on. There are 76 units in this book, 18 per term plus four Review and Test units. Each term is divided into the four areas of knowledge that need to be understood and learned in order to develop a comprehensive mastery of spelling:

Phonological Knowledge — how words sound

Word Function Knowledge — how word function can change spelling

Meaning Knowledge — how context can change word form

Word History Knowledge — how words have been derived

The Phonological Knowledge and the Word Function Knowledge sections include Revision and Test sheets for each term. Four units of Review and Test sheets covering the whole book are provided at the end of Term 4.

This book also contains useful tools to support students with their spelling. At the back of the book you'll find:

★ Useful Words list

★ WINK: Words I Need to Know — space to record problematic words

★ Some Tips for Learning to Spell

★ Assessment checklist

★ Glossary of Terms

Answers to all activities are provided in a special liftout section. A useful **topic list** for the whole year is given before the units.

Spelling Success provides an integrated method of teaching phonics, spelling and vocabulary. These books will improve literacy skills through effective instruction and evaluation based on the latest research into how spelling is best taught and learned successfully.

Book 3 Topic Chart

Long a sound patterns

The long a sound can be spelled in different ways, in **baby, whale** and **chain.**

A Write each word from the box in its correct sentence.

baby
daisy
sailor
waiter
safety
plate
tame
snake

1. I asked the ______________ to bring me a serviette.
2. Riley picked the ______________ and put it in a vase.
3. When I finished the meal I put my knife and fork on the ______________.
4. When the storm began we ran for the ______________ of the cave.
5. The wild dog is now ______________ and you can pat it.
6. The poisonous ______________ slithered under the log.
7. The mother gently laid the ______________ in its cradle.
8. The ______________ hurried back to her ship before it sailed.

B Join the word pieces in the boxes to make words that have the meanings on the right and write them on the lines.

h	**ake**
wh	**ace**
st	**ale**
r	**ave**
c	**able**
br	**ane**
f	**age**
pl	**ate**

1. large ocean creature ______________
2. dislike ______________
3. home of a horse ______________
4. garden tool ______________
5. where birds may be kept ______________
6. very courageous ______________
7. the front of something ______________
8. flying machine ______________

C Write these words in sentences of your own:

table ______________________________

skate______________________________

Parent/Teacher Signature Date

UNIT 2

Short a sound patterns

The letter a can make a short a sound, as in **bat** and **apple**.

A Write each word from the box in its correct sentence.

sand	1. Oliver hit the nail into the wood with a ______________.
hammer	2. I ate a juicy red ______________ for lunch.
apple	3. Mia climbed up the tall ______________ carefully.
ladder	4. The magician showed us some ______________ tricks.
magic	5. The ______________ of the tree could be seen on a sunny day.
shadow	6. In the desert the ______________ bloomed at night.
tadpole	7. After a few weeks the ______________ turned into a frog.
cactus	8. She made a ______________ castle at the beach.

B The short a words in the box have been cramped up. Write them in the spaces below.

splashmatchcatchcamelwagonbatterhappenfancy

1. ______________ 5. ______________

2. ______________ 6. ______________

3. ______________ 7. ______________

4. ______________ 8. ______________

C Write these words in sentences of your own:

badge ______________________________

bank ______________________________

Parent/Teacher Signature Date

Long e sound patterns

The long e sound can be spelled in different ways, as in **these** (e + e), **feet** (ee), **easy** (ea) and **chief** (ie).

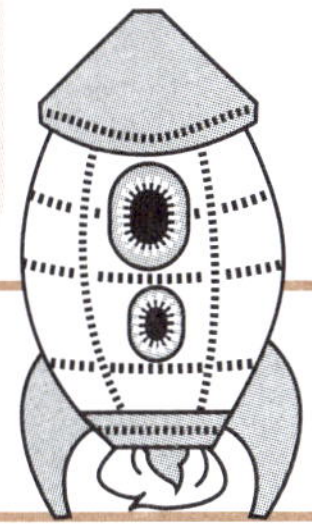

A Find the long e words in the grid and write them beside their meanings.

e	v	e	n	i	n	g
s	t	h	e	s	e	n
q	w	h	e	e	l	i
u	q	u	e	e	n	e
e	c	r	e	e	k	c
a	s	h	e	e	p	e
k	f	r	e	e	z	e

1. animals that produce wool ________________
2. female royalty ________________
3. the ones you want ________________
4. early night time ________________
5. noise of a mouse ________________
6. small stream ________________
7. female relation ________________
8. a thing that turns ________________
9. to turn water into ice ________________

B Write each long e word from the box in its correct sentence.

steam
here
weak
scene
dream
fleas
teeth
sweet

1. After her operation Sophie felt quite ________________.
2. Jack cleans his ________________ after each meal.
3. A lot of ________________ was coming off the boiling water.
4. The teacher ordered the children to come ________________.
5. The tea with all that sugar tasted ________________.
6. The artist painted a ________________ of the ocean.
7. Last night I had a ________________ about dinosaurs.
8. We sprayed our puppy to kill all the ________________.

C Draw a picture of each of these long e words.

feet	geese	peach	concrete

Parent/Teacher Signature   Date

UNIT 4

Short e sound patterns

The short e sound can also be made using different spellings, as in **them**, **shelf** and **dead**.

A Find the short e words in this row of cramped-up words and write them beside their meanings below.

tennisweptbreadcentdeaddrencheggsleft

1. cried ____________
2. unit of money ____________
3. to soak with water ____________
4. what birds lay ____________
5. the opposite of right ____________
6. a sport ____________
7. a food made from flour ____________
8. not alive ____________

B The short e words in the brackets have their letters jumbled. Write the correct word in each sentence.

1. When the sun came out the snow began to ______________. (mlet)
2. Chloe and I sit at the same ______________ at school. (dske)
3. The boys ate so many lollies there was only one ______________. (lfte)
4. She drew a ______________ of a dog in her book. (skchte)
5. The miners crushed the rock to get the ______________. (leda)
6. I stacked all the books on the ______________. (shlfe)
7. Those cakes are ______________ but these are stale. (frshe)
8. Lily ______________ the floor with the straw broom. (swpte)

C Write these short e words in sentences of your own:

petal ____

pencil ____

gem ____

Parent/Teacher Signature   Date

Long i sound patterns

The letter i can make a long i sound, as in **icy** and **high**.

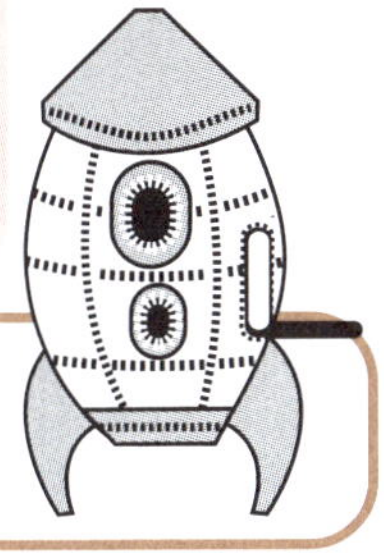

A Write each long i word from the box beside a word it can be linked to in some way below.

pirate	**spider**	**pilot**	**hive**
pile	**white**	**crime**	**knife**

1. aeroplane ____________
2. bee ____________
3. detective ____________
4. treasure ____________
5. black ____________
6. web ____________
7. fork ____________
8. heap ____________

B Write each long i word from the box beside its opposite below.

like	**alive**	**smile**	**bright**
wise	**silent**	**tighten**	**higher**

1. frown ____________
2. stupid ____________
3. dead ____________
4. loosen ____________
5. noisy ____________
6. lower ____________
7. hate ____________
8. dull ____________

C Unjumble the letters and write the correct word on the line.

1. vhie ____________
2. regti ____________
3. kebi ____________
2. derspi ____________

Parent/Teacher Signature   Date

Short i sound patterns

The letter i often makes a short i sound, as in **bit** and **disc**.

A Write these short i words in their correct sentences below.

river	**visit**	**picnic**	**winter**
fifty	**sister**	**hiss**	**swift**

1. The family went to the park for a ________________.
2. The snow began to fall in the ________________ months.
3. A snail is slow but a deer is a ________________ runner.
4. The number after forty-nine is ________________.
5. The children caught seven fish in the ________________.
6. My ________________, Charlotte, works as a mechanic.
7. The snake began to ________________ when we got close to it.
8. We are going to ________________ our friends in Perth next week.

B Use the word endings from the box to complete the short i words below to match the pictures.

ger	**er**	**ow**	**ney**
ow	**er**	**en**	**en**

1.  chim______	**2.**  fin______	**3.** 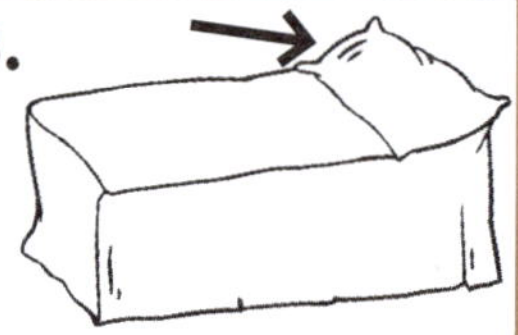 pill______	**4.**  mitt______
5.  dinn______	**6.**  kitt______	**7.**  slipp______	**8.**  wind______

Parent/Teacher Signature Date

Revision

A Write the words from the box under their correct sounds below.

apple	snake	tadpole	baby
tame	hammer	plate	splash

Long a words ______ ______ ______ ______

Short a words ______ ______ ______ ______

B Write the words from the box under their correct headings below.

here	sketch	dead	squeak
desk	scene	sheep	fresh

Long e words ______ ______ ______ ______

Short e words ______ ______ ______ ______

C Write the words from the box under their correct headings below.

finger	icy	kitten	high
crime	fist	spice	sister

Long i words ______ ______ ______ ______

Short i words ______ ______ ______ ______

Parent/Teacher Signature Date

Test 1

Choose the correct spelling of the word in brackets. Write the correct word in the space.

1	The (babby, baby) was sleeping in the cot.	1
2	The (snake, snacke) nearly bit her on the leg.	2
3	Ella ate a delicious (apple, appel) for lunch.	3
4	We need to all (faice, face) the front.	4
5	The water soon began to (freese, freeze).	5
6	William felt (week, weak) after his illness.	6
7	I ate a slice of (brerd, bread) for lunch.	7
8	She drew a (skech, sketch) in her book.	8
9	The (spider, spidar) spun a large web.	9
10	After the explosion everything was (sighlent, silent).	10
11	In (winter, winta) it often rains.	11
12	Melbourne is a large (sity, city).	12

Total correct ______ / 12

Parent/Teacher Signature　　　　Date

Test 2

The underlined words are spelled wrongly. Write the correct spelling in the space.

1	The <u>wayter</u> brought us our meal.	1
2	We saw a <u>whail</u> in the ocean.	2
3	Lachlan put the nails in with a <u>hamer</u>.	3
4	What time did the accident <u>hapen</u>?	4
5	Her <u>neice</u> Sally lives in Geelong.	5
6	I had a scary <u>dreem</u> last night.	6
7	The boy <u>weped</u> when his mother left.	7
8	I have a ten-<u>sent</u> coin to spend.	8
9	The team colours are black and <u>wite</u>.	9
10	I used a spanner to <u>titen</u> the nuts.	10
11	A large, wide <u>riva</u> flows through the valley.	11
12	We will <u>viset</u> our friends next week.	12

Total correct ______ / 12

Parent/Teacher Signature

Date

Plurals, adding s

Plural means more than one. Most naming words (nouns) make their plural simply by adding s.
Examples: one dog, five dogs; one house, six houses

A Add s to make the words in the boxes mean more than one. Draw a picture for each one.

1.

one tree three ________________

2.

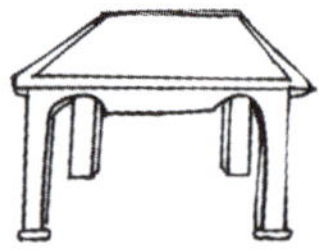

one table two ________________

3.

one flower many ________________

4.

one bird several ________________

B Make the words in brackets mean more than one.

1. I filled the three ______________________ with water. (bottle)
2. There were several ______________________ in the classroom. (girl)
3. I read five ______________________ last week. (book)
4. I bought some ______________________ to school for our class party. (cake)
5. We have ten ______________________ in our classroom. (computer)
6. There are two ______________________ in our town. (supermarket)
7. We have lots of bright ______________________ in our house. (light)
8. The children must take off their ______________________ before coming inside. (hat)

Parent/Teacher Signature Date

UNIT 11

Plurals, words ending in sh and ch

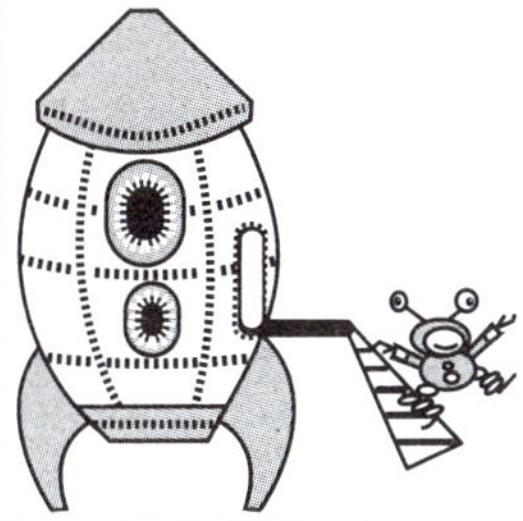

To make the plurals (more than one) of words that end in ch or sh you add es. Examples: one rash, several rashes; one witch, three witches

A Add es to the word in the boxes to make it mean more than one. Draw a picture for each one.

1.

one peach two ______________

2.

one dish four ______________

3.

one bush three ______________

4.

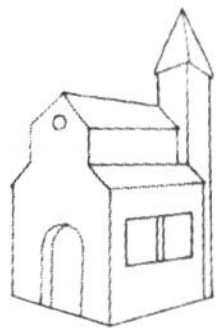

one church five ______________

B Add es to the words in brackets to complete each sentence.

1. During the cricket match Emily took three ______________. (catch)
2. I had to sew ten ______________ in my torn shorts. (stitch)
3. The genie gave the children three ______________. (wish)
4. There were seven large ______________ in the garden. (bush)
5. A lot of ______________ have happened at this corner. (crash)
6. Ethan's father owns six ______________. (watch)
7. There are a lot of football ______________ to be played this year. (match)
8. In the fairy story there were two evil ______________. (witch)

Parent/Teacher Signature Date

UNIT 12

Plurals, words ending in s, ss, x and z

To make the plurals of words that end in s, ss, x and z you add es.
Examples: one gas, several gases; one glass, a tray of glasses; one box, three boxes, one buzz, many buzzes

A Make the words in the boxes plural by adding es. Draw a picture for each one.

1. 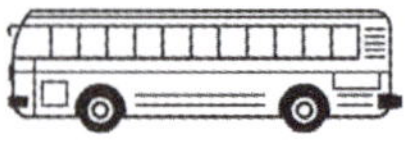 one bus two __________	**2.**  one fox two __________
3.  one box three __________	**4.**  one dress two __________

B Add es to make the words in brackets mean more than one. Write them in the spaces.

1. Oxygen and nitrogen are two common __________. (gas)
2. Ella has many __________ to wear. (dress)
3. Lots of __________ broke when the box dropped. (glass)
4. The teacher gave me three __________. (guess)
5. We sent seven __________ yesterday. (fax)
6. My brother has two different __________ to work for. (boss)
7. We could hear all the __________ coming from the bees. (buzz)
8. During the netball game Olivia had lots of successful __________. (pass)

Parent/Teacher Signature Date

Plurals, words ending ay, ey and oy

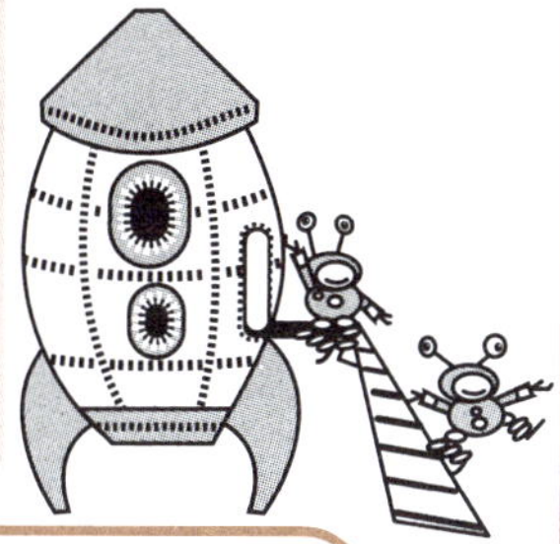

To make the plurals of words that end in ay, ey and oy you simply adding s. Examples: one day, two days; one donkey, three donkeys; one boy, many boys

A Make the words in the boxes plural by adding s. Draw a picture for each one.

1. 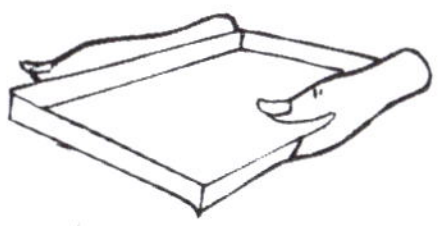 one tray two ________________	**2.**  one monkey two ________________
3.  one key four ________________	**4.**  one toy three ________________

B Make the words in brackets mean more than one. Write them in the spaces.

1. We have been on two ______________________ this year. (holiday)
2. At the beach a lady had five ______________________. (donkey)
3. There are lots of ______________________ in the room. (boy)
4. I saw over one hundred ______________________ at the supermarket. (trolley)
5. We have two ______________________ in our bodies. (kidney)
6. There are only ten ______________________ until my birthday. (day)
7. On Melbourne Cup day I saw lots of ______________________. (jockey)
8. This farm has hundreds of ______________________. (turkey)

Parent/Teacher Signature Date

UNIT 14

Revision

A Write the words from the box under their headings below. Make each word mean more than one.

pen	**box**	**dish**	**toy**
gas	**beach**	**bush**	**guess**
turkey	**coin**	**tray**	**bird**

+ s		+ es	
______	______	______	______
______	______	______	______
______	______	______	______

B Make each of these words mean more than one (plural). The first one has been done for you.

One	More than one	One	More than one
1. boy	*boys*	5. match	______
2. jockey	______	6. branch	______
3. brush	______	7. peach	______
4. pet	______	8. dress	______

C Change these words to plural and write them in a sentence.

1. donkey ______________________
2. beach ______________________
3. apple ______________________
4. bus ______________________

Parent/Teacher Signature Date

Test

The underlined words are spelled wrongly. Write the correct spelling in the space.

1	I have six different coloured <u>penciles</u>.	1
2	There are a lot of <u>shopes</u> in our city.	2
3	There are lots of <u>bushs</u> in our garden.	3
4	There are seven <u>busses</u> in the carpark.	4
5	Michelle has lots of <u>dreses</u> to wear.	5
6	There were five <u>monkies</u> in the tree.	6
7	We saw two <u>donkies</u> at the beach.	7
8	I tried four different <u>keyes</u> to open the door.	8
9	There are lots and lots of <u>glasess</u> on the table.	9
10	My pets are three cuddly <u>catts</u>.	10
11	There are several <u>wayes</u> you can go to Sydney.	11
12	The fairy princess gave the children three <u>wishs</u>.	12

Total correct ______
12

Parent/Teacher Signature Date

Compound words 1

Compound words are made up of two or more smaller words. Examples: any + thing = anything; some + where = somewhere

A Complete each compound word by adding a word from the box to the blanks below. Draw a picture of each one.

hopper	**fall**	**port**	**fish**
mill	**path**	**berry**	**brush**

1. star__________	**2.** car__________	**3.** water__________	**4.** grass__________
5. tooth__________	**6.** straw__________	**7.** foot__________	**8.** wind__________

B Unjumble the letters of the words at the top and write them in the spaces to form compound words. Draw a picture of each one.

1. dgo bull__________	**2.** btoa tug__________	**3.** abll foot__________	**4.** isde sea__________
5. fshi jelly__________	**6.** ctoa over__________	**7.** rfie camp__________	**8.** wkor home__________

Parent/Teacher Signature Date

Compound words 2

Compound words are made up of two or more smaller words. Examples: any + thing = anything; some + where = somewhere

A Add a word from the box to complete each compound word below.

ball	**chair**	**box**	**paste**
yard	**board**	**lace**	**roads**

1. I got all the letters in the mail____________.
2. I cleaned my teeth with the new tooth____________.
3. I fell asleep in the big arm____________.
4. Tom, my friend, likes to play base____________.
5. The accident happened at the cross____________.
6. The teacher wrote our spelling on the white____________.
7. We like to play cricket in the back____________.
8. Mia wore the neck____________ her mother gave her.

B Choose a word from the box to complete each compound word. Draw a picture for each one.

1. free________	**2.** basket________	**3.** table________	**4.** egg________	**stack** **shoe** **box** **cup**
5. butter________	**6.** match________	**7.** horse________	**8.** hay________	**cloth** **way** **ball** **fly**

Parent/Teacher Signature Date

Word groups

Nouns are naming words for places, people and things. You can group nouns together that are the names of certain things, like different foods or sports.

A Sort the words in the box under their headings below.

rice	bean	apple	lettuce
cherry	wheat	oats	barley
carrot	grape	cabbage	peach

Vegetables **Fruit** **Cereal grains**

______ ______ ______ ______ ______ ______

______ ______ ______ ______ ______ ______

B Sort the words in the box under their headings below.

car	square	van	oblong
triangle	badminton	rectangle	cricket
tennis	truck	football	motorbike

Shapes **Sports** **Vehicles**

______ ______ ______ ______ ______ ______

______ ______ ______ ______ ______ ______

C Sort the words in the box under their headings below.

bathroom	rocket	sink	planet
seeds	carpet	comet	flowers
star	hose	hoe	cupboard

Space **Garden** **Home**

______ ______ ______ ______ ______ ______

______ ______ ______ ______ ______ ______

Parent/Teacher Signature Date

Long o sound patterns

The letter o is sometimes pronounced as a long o sound, as in **soda** and **woke**.

A Find the long o words in the grid and write each beside its meaning.

b	o	n	e	s	f
c	p	o	n	y	r
l	r	o	s	e	o
o	d	o	z	e	z
s	t	o	e	s	e
e	n	o	s	e	n

1. digits on your feet ________________
2. small horse ________________
3. flower ________________
4. dogs like to eat them ________________
5. to sleep ________________
6. near ________________
7. turned to ice ________________
8. a feature on your face ________________

B Add a word piece from the box to complete the words in the sentences below.

work	**ter**	**ly**	**age**
er	**en**	**ate**	**ful**

1. The new toy is already brok________.
2. The wealthy lady will don________ some money to the charity.
3. Our teacher gave us some home________ last night.
4. We are hope________ that the lost dog will be found.
5. I bought five post________ stamps this morning.
6. I put the slices of bread in the toas________.
7. Sam cut the thick grass with the mow________.
8. When everyone had left he felt quite lone________.

C These long o words have been written backwards. Write them correctly on the lines.

1. afos ________ 2. naeco ________ 3. epor ________ 4. rotom ________

Parent/Teacher Signature Date

UNIT 20

Short o sound patterns

The letter o can also make a short o sound, as in **odd** and **block**.

A Find the words in the cramped-up row and write each beside a word it can be linked to in some way below.

golfclockdollarstoppocketsoftfrogknob

1. cent ____________
2. shirt ____________
3. handle ____________
4. toad ____________
5. sport ____________
6. hard ____________
7. time ____________
8. halt ____________

B Find the short o words in the grid and write each in the correct sentence below.

b	l	o	s	t	d
o	m	o	t	h	o
t	s	h	o	p	c
t	p	o	n	d	t
l	l	o	c	k	o
e	c	r	o	p	r

1. We bought some lollies at the ____________.
2. I saw some tadpoles in the ____________.
3. I have ____________ all my money.
4. The ____________ flew around the room.
5. You must ________ the door before going out.
6. I drank a full ____________ of water.
7. The ____________ listened to my heart beat.
8. The farmer is planting a new ____________.

C Unjumble these short o words and write them in sentences of your own.

1. tosh ____

2. gnol ____

Parent/Teacher Signature Date

Long u sound patterns

The letter u can be sounded as a long u, as in **cute** and **pupil**.

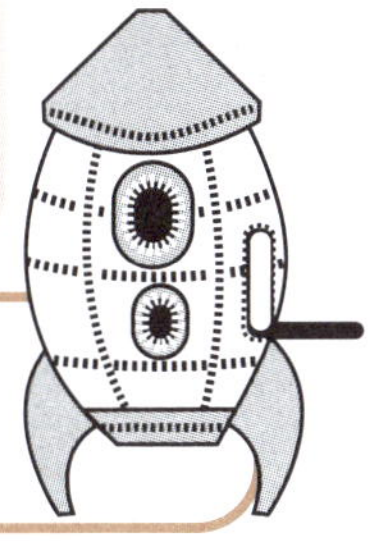

A Find each of the long u words in this cramped up word line and write them in the correct sentences below.

tunehugetulipmusicstudentcutetubefumes

1. We had to ________________ the guitar before we could play it.
2. Ethan has been a ________________ at our school for five years.
3. The ________________ from the petrol tank are very strong.
4. Ruby can be very ________________ when she wants to.
5. Riley planted some ________________ bulbs in the garden.
6. An elephant is a ________________ animal.
7. We listened to the ________________ on my radio.
8. The water ran through the ________________.

B Write each long u word from the box beside its meaning below.

bugle	**perfume**	**mule**	**cube**
rescue	**picture**	**beauty**	**cure**

1. musical instrument ________________
2. a horse-like animal ________________
3. sweet-smelling scent ________________
4. a shape ________________
5. to heal a disease ________________
6. lovely to look at ________________
7. save ________________
8. drawing or painting ________________

C Write each of these short u words in a sentence of your own:

value ________________________________

pure ________________________________

Parent/Teacher Signature Date

UNIT 22

Short u sound patterns

The letter **u** can also be pronounced as a short **u** sound, as in **cut** and **such**.

A Add a word piece from the box to complete the short **u** words below to match its picture.

ton	**nel**	**fly**	**ire**
py	**et**	**el**	**um**

1.  fun______	**2.**  but______	**3.**  butter______	**4.**  ump______
5.  pup______	**6.**  buck______	**7.**  tunn______	**8.** 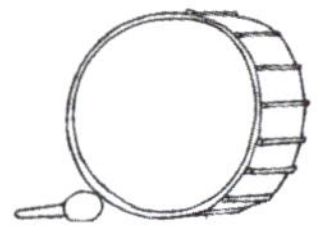 dr______

B Write each word from the box in its correct sentence.

crust
buzz
plug
number
supper
under
puzzle
ugly

1. I put the ______________________ in the bath to stop the water escaping.
2. I ate the thick ______________________ of the bread.
3. We ate some crumpets for ______________________ last night.
4. The teacher helped Jack and I solve the ______________________.
5. I could hear the ______________________ of the bees outside.
6. One thousand is a large ______________________.
7. The wicked witch in the fairy story was quite ______________________.
8. I found my lost watch ______________________ the bed.

C Write each of these short **u** words in sentences of your own:

munch ____

pump ____

Parent/Teacher Signature   Date

r-Influenced vowels, ar

When the letter **a** is followed by an **r**, the **a** is pronounced like a long **ar** sound, as in **far** and **car**.

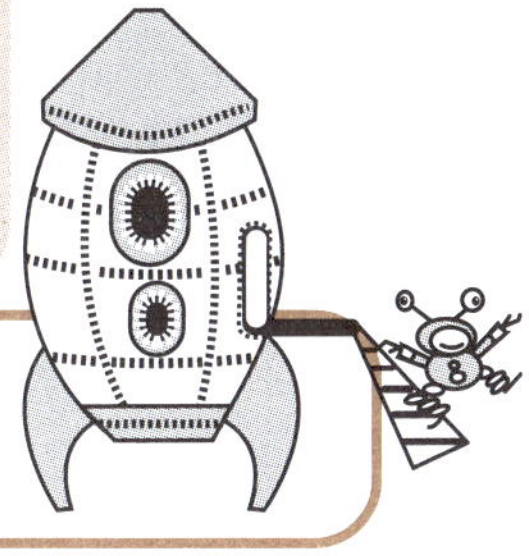

A The **ar** words below are written backwards. Write them correctly and draw a picture for each one.

1. drac ________	**2.** trac ________	**3.** krahs ________	**4.** krap ________
5. raj ________	**6.** rats ________	**7.** nedrag ________	**8.** prah ________

B Write each **ar** word from the box in its correct sentence below.

march	**large**	**bark**	**dark**
spark	**artist**	**target**	**sharp**

1. A ______________ from the fire set the paper alight.
2. The blade of this knife is very ______________.
3. A mouse is small but an elephant is ______________.
4. The archer hit a bullseye on the ______________.
5. The ______________ painted a picture of the ocean.
6. The soldiers started to ______________ along the road.
7. We could hear the dog ______________ from a long way away.
8. It's light now but it will soon be ______________.

C Write these **ar** words in sentences of your own:

farmer ____

scarf ____

Parent/Teacher Signature Date

r-Influenced vowels, ur

When the letter u is followed by an r, it is pronounced as a long er sound, as in **fur** and **turn**.

A Find the ur words in the grid and write each one in its correct sentence.

r	b	u	r	n	c
e	p	u	r	r	h
t	s	u	r	f	u
u	s	p	u	r	r
r	h	u	r	t	c
n	h	u	r	l	h

1. My kitten began to _____________ when I patted it.
2. When Cooper fell he _____________ his hand.
3. The cowboy dug the __________ into the horse's side.
4. The paper began to _____________ when it was lit.
5. She attends _____________ every Sunday.
6. We took our boards down to the __________ beach.
7. I don't know if she will ever _________________.
8. She began to _________ the weight across the oval.

B Choose the correct ur word from the brackets to write in the spaces.

1. If you blow up a balloon it might (burn, burst) ______________.
2. I spoke to a (nurse, purse) ______________ at the hospital.
3. The colour of this paper is (purple, further) ______________.
4. I put all the coins in my (purse, nurse) ______________.
5. The grass on the hill has been (curve, burned) ______________.
6. There was a (certain, curtain) ______________ over the window.
7. I am going to (curl, hurl) ______________ her long hair.
8. The car crashed into the (curb, purr) ______________ of the street.

C Write these ur words in sentences of your own:

burr ____

curve ____

Parent/Teacher Signature Date

Revision

UNIT 25

A Sort the words in the box under the headings below.

bone	pocket	rope	clock
moth	sofa	frog	postage

Long o words ______ ______ ______ ______

Short o words ______ ______ ______ ______

B Sort the words in the box under the headings below.

tulip	huge	butter	tune
button	thunder	pure	umpire

Long u words ______ ______ ______ ______

Short u words ______ ______ ______ ______

C Add ar or ur to complete each word in the box and then write them under the headings below.

p____r	ch____ch	h____m	h____t
f____m	sc____	b____st	c____t

ar words ______ ______ ______ ______

ur words ______ ______ ______ ______

Parent/Teacher Signature   Date

Test 1

Choose the correct spelling of the word in brackets. Write the correctly spelled word in the space.

1	I picked a (roze, rose) from the garden.	1
2	We cooked the bread in the (toaster, toasta).	2
3	I filled the (bottle, botel) with oil.	3
4	I put a key in my (poket, pocket).	4
5	I like to listen to (muzik, music) on the radio.	5
6	Mia gave me a bottle of (purfume, perfume).	6
7	I spread the (butta, butter) on the bread.	7
8	I tried to solve the difficult (puzzle, pussle).	8
9	I saw the (starr, star) twinkling in the sky.	9
10	He fired the gun and hit the (target, tarjet).	10
11	Do you think she will (retern, return) today?	11
12	After the play we closed the (curtin, curtain).	12

Total correct ______
12

Parent/Teacher Signature Date

Test 2

The underlined words are spelled wrongly. Write them correctly in the space.

1	The dog ate the boune.	1
2	The teacher gave us some homwork last night.	2
3	The clok on the ledge is ten minutes slow.	3
4	My mother took me to see the docter.	4
5	Ella played a great tuen on the piano.	5
6	The workers tried to rescoo the trapped kitten.	6
7	I filled the buckat with water.	7
8	We had scones for a late night suppa.	8
9	We watched the starte of the race.	9
10	It was darrk when we got home.	10
11	If you strike it the match will bern.	11
12	Sophie berst the balloon.	12

Total correct ______
12

Parent/Teacher Signature Date

UNIT 28

Plurals, words ending in y

Plural means more than one. To make the plural of words that end in **y** after a consonant, you change the **y** to **i** and then add **es**. Example: cry, cries

A Make the words in the boxes plural by changing the **y** to **i** and then adding **es**. Draw pictures for each one.

1.  one fly two ________________	**2.**  one lady three ________________
3.  one pony two ________________	**4.**  one poppy three ________________

B Make the words in brackets plural by adding **es**. Don't forget to change the **y** to **i**.

1. There are lots of ______________________ in Australia. (city)
2. Our teacher told us five ______________________ yesterday. (story)
3. I ate all the ______________________ we picked. (berry)
4. Our town has two different ______________________. (library)
5. The teacher gave us all two ______________________ each. (diary)
6. Joshua has lots of different ______________________. (hobby)
7. There were many ______________________ at the clinic. (baby)
8. My father made us two flavoured ______________________. (jelly)

Parent/Teacher Signature Date

Adding ed, no change

You often need to add ed to the ends of words to make sure they fit correctly in a sentence. Sometimes there is no change to the spelling of the base word. Example: We will look for the puppy later. Yesterday we looked for the puppy.

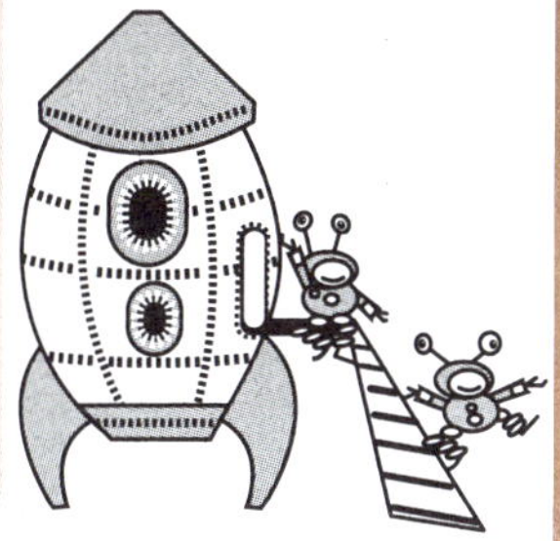

A Make each underlined word end in ed and write it in the second sentence.

1. Today I will ask the teacher. Yesterday I ______________ the teacher.
2. Today I will play football. Yesterday I ______________ football.
3. Today I will show them my bicycle. Yesterday I ______________ my bicycle to them.
4. Today I will cook bacon and eggs. Yesterday I ______________ bacon and eggs.

B Make the words in brackets end in ed so they fit the meaning of the sentence.

1. The plane ______________ on the tarmac last week. (land)
2. We ______________ everywhere for the missing puppy this morning. (look)
3. When they were late yesterday the boys ______________ to the room. (rush)
4. The story the teacher read us ______________ happily. (end)
5. The farmer ______________ his cows last night. (milk)
6. Yesterday the driver ______________ the car into the wall. (back)
7. The explorers ______________ in the tents last night. (camp)
8. Oliver ______________ lots of trees along the creek bed. (plant)

Parent/Teacher Signature Date

UNIT 30

Adding ing, no change

You often need to add ing to the ends of words to make sure they fit correctly in a sentence. Sometimes there is no change to the spelling of the base word. Example: We will look for the puppy later. Today we are looking for the puppy.

A Make the words in brackets end in ing and write them on the lines.

1. The girls are ________________ for a fine day. (wish)
2. The boy is ________________ up for the disco. (dress)
3. The chicks are ________________ from the eggs. (hatch)
4. Chloe is ________________ the ball. (kick)
5. The birds are ________________ across the forest. (fly)
6. The choir is ________________ a popular song. (sing)

B Make the words in the brackets end in ing and write them in the spaces. Draw a picture for each one.

1.	**2.**	**3.**
Tom is ________________ in the river. (fish)	Jack is ________________ the clothes. (wash)	Ella is ________________ the weight. (lift)
4.	**5.**	**6.**
The cat is ________________ its fur. (lick)	Tom is ________________ a hamburger. (eat)	The teacher is ________________ us a story. (read)

Parent/Teacher Signature Date

Adding ed or ing, doubling letters

For words that end in a short vowel and a consonant you double the last letter before adding ed or ing. Example: Tomorrow I will pin the chart on the wall. Yesterday I pinned the chart on the wall. Today I am pinning the chart on the wall.

A Make the underlined word in the boxes end in ed. Don't forget to double the last consonant. Draw a picture for each one.

1. I will chop the wood. I ____________ the wood yesterday.	**2.** I will pat the dog. I ____________ the dog before.
3. Mary, don't drop the ball. Mary ____________ the ball.	**4.** I need to rub my leg. I ____________ my leg when it hurt.

B Make the words in brackets end in ing. Don't forget to double the last letter.

1. The car is ________________ at the corner. (stop)
2. The audience was ________________ loudly at the end of the concert. (clap)
3. The lion is ________________ the zebra to its lair. (drag)
4. I am ________________ our classroom party. (plan)
5. My mother is ________________ for mushrooms before lunch. (shop)
6. The boat is ________________ over the waves. (skip)
7. The boys are ________________ the room for us this morning. (mop)
8. The frog is ________________ across the road. (hop)

Parent/Teacher Signature　　　　　　　　　　Date

UNIT 32

Revision

A Change the words in the box to plurals. Write them under the correct headings below.

boy	**toy**	**story**	**donkey**
baby	**fly**	**army**	**poppy**
city	**holiday**	**monkey**	**key**

+ s

Change y to i + es

______ ______ ______ ______

______ ______ ______ ______

______ ______ ______ ______

B Add ed to the words below and write them under their headings below.

stop	**scrub**	**ask**	**mop**
play	**shock**	**clap**	**plan**
fish	**rub**	**camp**	**rush**

+ ed

Double last letter + ed

______ ______ ______ ______

______ ______ ______ ______

______ ______ ______ ______

C Make these words end in ing and write each in a sentence of your own.

1. plant ______
2. wish ______
3. drop ______
4. mop ______

Parent/Teacher Signature Date

Test

Choose the correct spelling of the words in brackets.
Write them in the spaces.

1	There are several (blowflys, blowflies) on the food.	1
2	We picked lots of (berrys, berries) from the bush.	2
3	My dad made us lots of (jellies, jellys).	3
4	The teacher read us two (stories, storys).	4
5	I (looked, lookt) everywhere for the lost puppy.	5
6	The scouts (campt, camped) in some tents.	6
7	The farmer has (milkt, milked) the cows.	7
8	Noah (choped, chopped) up all the wood.	8
9	The teacher (dragged, draged) the desk to the room.	9
10	I (rubed, rubbed) my leg because it was itchy.	10
11	Sophie is (liften, lifting) the weight.	11
12	Jack is (reading, readen) a comic.	12

Total correct ________
12

Parent/Teacher Signature Date

UNIT 34

Homophones 1

Homophones are words that sound the same but have different spellings and different meanings.
Examples: some (several), sum (addition); hour (60 minutes), our (belonging to us)

A Write the word that matches each picture.

1. pair, pear	2. bean, been	3. ball, bawl	4. ate, eight
 ____________	 ____________	 ____________	 ____________
5. sea, see	**6.** tow, toe	**7.** flour, flower	**8.** rose, rows
 ____________	 ____________	 ____________	 ____________

B Write each word from the box in its correct sentence below.

deer	**steel**	**week**	**fir**
dear	**steal**	**weak**	**fur**

1. The thief tried to ____________ the diamond.
2. A large ____________ tree grew in the forest.
3. There is only a ____________ to go before my birthday.
4. After her operation Mia felt quite ____________.
5. The wolves ran after the ____________ and its fawn.
6. This device is made of stainless ____________.
7. There seemed to be a lot fleas in the ____________ of the dog.
8. These shoes are cheap but the ones on that table are ____________.

Parent/Teacher Signature Date

Homophones 2

Homophones are words that sound the same but have different spellings and different meanings. Examples: some (several), sum (addition); hour (60 minutes), our (belonging to us)

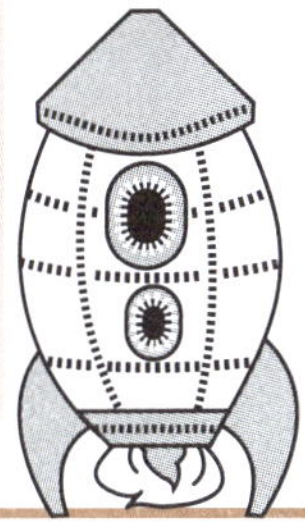

A Find the words in the grid and write each beside its homophone.

p	e	a	r	o	s
r	a	i	n	n	e
m	a	i	l	e	e
f	l	o	w	e	r
t	o	e	s	u	n

1. rein ____________
2. won ____________
3. male ____________
4. tow ____________
5. pair ____________
6. sea ____________
7. flour ____________
8. son ____________

B These homophones are cramped up. Find each pair and write them together.

talewholecreakrodestairknewroadcreekstarenewholetail

1. ____________ ____________
2. ____________ ____________
3. ____________ ____________
4. ____________ ____________
5. ____________ ____________
6. ____________ ____________

C Write a homophone for these words.

1. plain ____________
2. rows ____________
3. been ____________
4. would ____________

Parent/Teacher Signature Date

UNIT 36

Words from the past

Many words we use come from ancient languages. The ancient words often give the base word that is used in different words today. Example: autos = self (autograph, automobile, automatic)

A Write the words from the box under the ancient words given with their meanings below. Draw a picture for each one.

television	**bicycle**	**graph**	**aquarium**
pedestrian	**dentist**	**asteroid**	**thermometer**

1. aqua = water ______________	**5.** grapho = I write ______________
2. cyclus = wheel ______________	**6.** meter = measure ______________
3. aster = a star ______________	**7.** dentis = tooth ______________
4. tele = I see from afar ______________	**8.** pedis = foot ______________

Parent/Teacher Signature　　　　　　　　　　Date

r–Influenced vowels, or, ore, our, oar

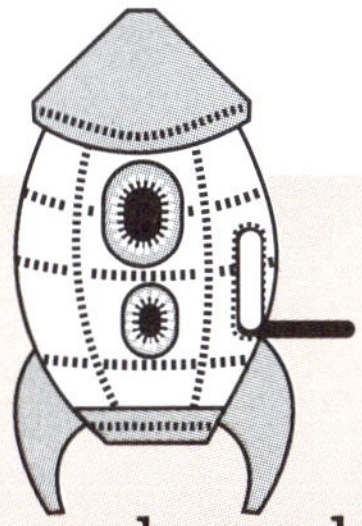

When the letter r follows different vowels it changes the way the word sounds. The word **fog** is pronounced with a short o sound but **for** is pronounced with a long vowel sound that we call an r-influenced vowel. Different letter patterns can make the same r-influenced vowel sound. Examples: born, bore, four, soar

A Find the or words in the grid. Write each in its correct sentence.

b	t	o	r	c	h	c
e	h	o	r	s	e	o
f	s	h	o	r	t	u
o	n	o	r	t	h	r
r	s	h	o	r	e	s
e	s	t	o	r	m	e

1. Josh is tall but Sam is ________________.
2. The cowboy put the saddle on the ______________.
3. The sailors in the wreck swam to the nearest _________.
4. I met Sally on the golf ________________.
5. I used a ________________ to see in the dark.
6. The violent ________________ wrecked many homes.
7. They went east then turned ________________.
8. We left ________________ he had arrived.

B Choose the correct word from the brackets to complete each sentence and write it on the line.

1. The farmer is harvesting the (corn, cord). ________________
2. The meat from a pig is called (fort, pork). ________________
3. Sally (wore, shore) her new clothes to school. ________________
4. I began to (pour, four) the water from the jug. ________________
5. I could hear the lion (boar, roar). ________________
6. Because it is light a (fork, cork) will float. ________________

Parent/Teacher Signature Date

UNIT 38

r–Influenced vowels, er, ear, eer

When the letter r follows different vowels it changes the way the word sounds. The word **hem** is pronounced with a short e sound but **her** is pronounced with a long vowel sound that we call an r-influenced vowel.

Different letter patterns can sometimes make the same r-influenced vowel sound, as in **her** and **heard**, or **beard** and **beer**. Sometimes the same letter patterns make different vowel sounds, as in **heard** and **beard**.

A Write the words from the box in their correct sentences.

deer
cheer
fern
verse
perch
learn
spear
year

1. Our teacher read the last ______________ of the poem.
2. The ______________ and its fawn walked through the leafy forest.
3. We ______________ how to do mathematics at school.
4. The crowd began to ______________ when he kicked the goal.
5. The man threw the ______________ at the fish.
6. A large tree ______________ grew in their backyard.
7. Next ______________ the teacher said I'd be in year four.
8. The fowls were roosting on the ______________ when the fox came by.

B Choose the correct word from the brackets and write it on the line.

1. In my garden I grew some (herds, herbs). ______________
2. The speeding car began to (swerve, clerk) across the road. ______________
3. The doctor listened to her (heart, head) beat. ______________
4. Dad asked me to (steer, sheer) the boat in the calm water. ______________
5. Mr James has a very long, bushy (bear, beard) on his chin. ______________
6. I could not (gear, hear) because of the thunder. ______________
7. Dad likes to drink a cold (beer, tear) on a hot day. ______________
8. Our class is going on an excursion this (germ, term). ______________

Parent/Teacher Signature   Date

r–Influenced vowels, ir, ire

When the letter r follows different vowels it changes the way the word sounds. The word **bid** is pronounced with a short i sound but **bird** is pronounced with a long vowel sound that we call an r-influenced vowel. If the letters ir are followed by an e, the word is pronounced with a different long vowel sound, as in **fire** and **shire**.

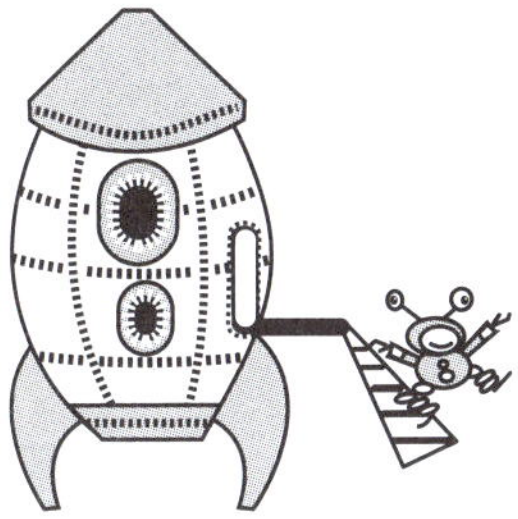

A Choose the word from the box to write under each picture.

skirt	**wire**	**first**	**shirt**
girl	**squirt**	**spire**	**circus**

1.  ________	**2.**  ________	**3.** 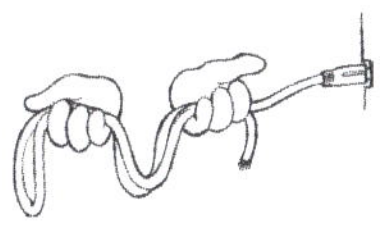 ________	**4.**  ________
5.  ________	**6.**  ________	**7.**  ________	**8.**  ________

B Choose the correct word in the brackets and write it on the line.

1. The number after twenty-nine is (thirsty, thirty). ________
2. I added the eggs and began to (stir, fir). ________
3. We bought some tickets to the (twirl, circus). ________
4. If you do not clean it the car becomes (thirty, dirty). ________
5. Jack is wearing a striped (shirt, birth) today. ________
6. The little boy got a lot of (third, dirt) on his face. ________
7. There are long pieces of (sire, wire) in this fence. ________
8. I am going to (hire, fire) a tent to camp in. ________

Parent/Teacher Signature Date

UNIT 40

Sound patterns, ow

The letters ow sometimes make an ow sound, as in **crowd**, and sometimes a long o sound, as in **throw**.

A Join a word piece from the box to the word piece in the sentence. These words are all pronounced with the ow sound, as in **cow**.

own	**ers**	**el**	**own**
er	**n**	**er**	**d**

1. Sally wore a long g__________ to the ball.
2. I dried myself with the tow__________.
3. I picked some flow__________ from the garden.
4. At the circus the cl__________ made us laugh.
5. There was a large crow__________ at the concert.
6. After we finished the race we had a show__________.
7. The queen wore a crow__________ on her head.
8. There is a tall tow__________ in our city.

B Complete each word to match its picture. These words are all pronounced with the long o sound, as in **yellow**. Say each word aloud.

1.  m______er	**2.** 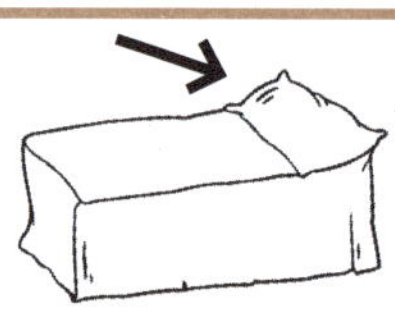 pill______	**3.**  sn______	**4.**  wind______
5. 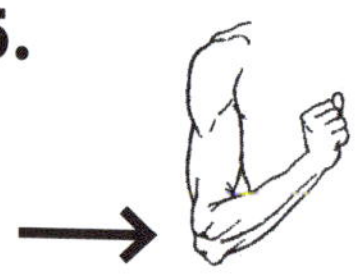 elb______	**6.**  r______ing	**7.**  shad______	**8.**  thr______ing

Parent/Teacher Signature Date

Sound patterns, long and short oo

The letters oo together can be pronounced as a long oo sound, as in **pool**, or they can be a short oo sound, as in **book**.

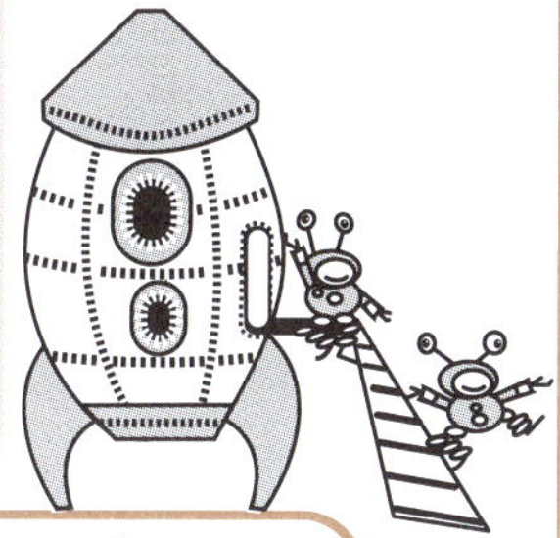

A Choose the correct word from the brackets to match each picture. Write it on the line. These words are all pronounced with the long o sound, as in **root**.

1. (noose, loose) 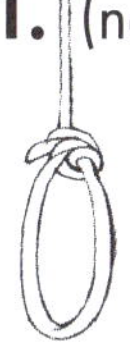 ________	**2.** (goose, boom)  ________	**3.** (troop, rooster)  ________	**4.** (cocoon, scoop) 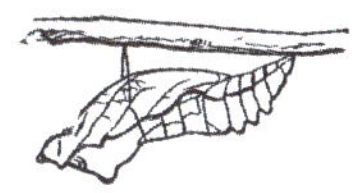 ________
5. (fool, stool)  ________	**6.** (rooster, hoop) 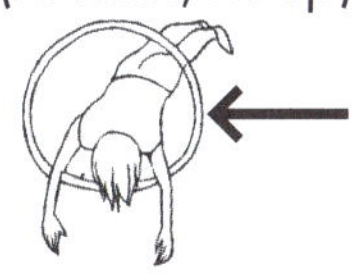 ________	**7.** (doom, snooze)  ________	**8.** (broom, smooth) 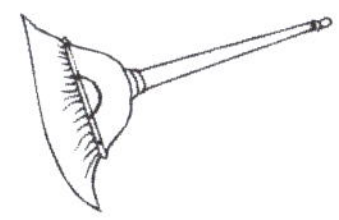 ________

B Write each word from the box in its correct sentence below. All these words are pronounced with the short oo sound, as in **look**.

wooden	**cooking**	**hood**	**book**
foot	**wool**	**shook**	**took**

1. Jack is ________ us a roast for lunch.
2. Chloe ________ her new puppy to school.
3. I read a ________ about dinosaurs yesterday.
4. Aiden has a ________ puppet in his room.
5. The explosion ________ our house.
6. The material has been made from the ________ of sheep.
7. The burglar wore a ________ to cover her face.
8. Sam hurt his ________ when he tripped over.

Parent/Teacher Signature Date

Sound patterns, oa and ou

The letters **oa** together are pronounced as a long **o** sound, as in **oats**. The letters **ou** together can be pronounced in different ways. They can be an **ow** sound, as in **spout**, a long **oo** sound as in **youth**, or a short **u** sound, as in **touch**.

A Find the **oa** words in the grid and write them in the space.

t	b	o	a	t	t
o	c	o	a	t	o
a	g	o	a	t	a
d	s	o	a	p	s
x	l	o	a	f	t
y	f	l	o	a	t

1. ____________ an item of clothing
2. ____________ a frog-like animal
3. ____________ a breakfast item
4. ____________ a sailing vessel
5. ____________ a farm animal
6. ____________ used to wash with
7. ____________ something that doesn't sink
8. ____________ how bread is baked

B Choose the correct word from the brackets and write it in the space. These words all use the letters **ou**.

1. I made the cake with (flour, flower) and eggs. ________________
2. A kangaroo has a (south, pouch) for its joey. ________________
3. To stay hidden he had to (crouch, couch) down low. ____________
4. I ate some tomato (youth, soup) for my lunch. ________________
5. My (cousin, courage) will visit me soon. ________________
6. Isabella (ground, found) the lost wallet. ________________
7. The opposite direction of north is (spout, south). ________________
8. The frightened boy began to (scout, shout) loudly. ________________

C Write these words in your own sentences:

hound ____

group ____

Parent/Teacher Signature   Date

Revision

UNIT 43

A Add or or er to the words in the box and write them under their headings below.

v____se	g____m	c____n	h____se
st____e	n____th	t____m	f____n

or

er

B Add ir or ow to the words in the box and write them under their headings below.

m____er	f____st	fl____er	sn____
b____d	pill____	squ____t	g____l

ir

ow

C Write the words in the box under their headings below.

goose	wood	stool	hood
foot	rooster	cook	snooze

long oo sound (tool)

short oo sound (book)

Parent/Teacher Signature

Date

UNIT 44

Test 1

The underlined words are spelled wrongly. Write the correct spelling in the space.

	Sentence	Answer
1	The shipwrecked sailor swam to the shure.	1
2	The cowboy rode the hause into town.	2
3	A large tree furn grew in the glasshouse.	3
4	The doctor listened to my hert beat.	4
5	An ostrich is a very large berd.	5
6	We are going to see the clowns at the cerkus.	6
7	I put the fhlour in the vase.	7
8	In our city there is a tall touer.	8
9	The nuts on the wheel gradually became luuse.	9
10	Sam has a woulden puppet.	10
11	I washed my dirty hands with sowp.	11
12	A kangaroo has a powch for its joey.	12

Total correct ______ / 12

Parent/Teacher Signature Date

Test 2

Choose the correct letter group from the brackets and write it ______________________ the space.

1 The violent st______m caused a lot of damage. (ur, or)

2 We could hear the lion r______. (ure, oar)

3 I made up the last v______se of the poem. (er, ur)

4 She is not sure what to w______ to the dance. (are, ear)

5 I was th______sty after the race. (er, ir)

6 I began to st______ all the contents in the bowl. (ir, ur)

7 The queen has a cr______n on her head. (aw, ow)

8 We cut the grass with a m______wer. (oo, ow)

9 At the farm we saw a g______se. (oo, ee)

10 Sophie is c______king dinner for us. (oo, uu)

11 We watched as it began to fl______t away. (ow, oa)

12 Jack had tomato s______p for lunch. (oo, ou)

Total correct ________
12

Parent/Teacher Signature   Date

UNIT 46

Adding ed, words ending in e

When you add ed to words that end in e, you drop the e before you add ed. Example: like + ed = liked

A Make these words end in ed. Write them in the spaces and draw a picture for each.

1. grate Tom ______________ the cheese for the pizza.	**2.** divide Sarah ______________ the lollies between them.	**3.** line Jack ______________ the box with paper.
4. dare Tom ______________ Jack to swim across the pool.	**5.** love I ______________ the circus last night.	**6.** hope He ______________ the test would be easy.

B Make these words end in ed. Remember to drop the e first.

1. face ______________
2. explode ______________
3. like ______________
4. erode ______________
5. lie ______________
6. dive ______________
7. rave ______________
8. fine ______________

C Write these words in sentences of your own:

skited ______________________________

typed ______________________________

Parent/Teacher Signature Date

Adding ing, words ending in e

For words that end in e, you drop the e before adding ing. Example: hope + ing = hoping

A Make these words end in ing. Write them in the spaces and draw a picture for each.

1. chase	**2.** race	**3.** bake
The dog is ______________ the cat.	The girls are ______________ across the yard.	Mike is ______________ a cake.
4. dance	**5.** wave	**6.** drive
The girls and boys are ______________.	Jack is ______________ to me.	Tom is ______________ the car.

B Make the word in brackets end in ing. Write them in the spaces.

1. The keeper is ______________ the zebra. (tame)
2. The children are ______________ the water. (waste)
3. The cows are ______________ in the paddock. (graze)
4. The fire is ______________ brightly. (blaze)
5. The students are ______________ pictures in their books. (paste)
6. Sam is ______________ a pair of pliers. (use)

Parent/Teacher Signature   Date

UNIT 48

Base words

A base word is a word that you can build other words from. Examples: brush (base word), brushed, brushing; hike (base word), hiked, hiking; swim (base word), swam, swimming

A Write the base word. The first one has been done for you.

1. watched comes from *watch*
2. kicked comes from ______
3. knocked comes from ______
4. wasted comes from ______
5. toasted comes from ______
6. lifted comes from ______
7. tricked comes from ______
8. rowed comes from ______

B Write the base word. The first one has been done for you.

1. tapped comes from *tap*
2. hopped comes from ______
3. skipped comes from ______
4. dropped comes from ______
5. smelled comes from ______
6. fanned comes from ______
7. filled comes from ______
8. stepped comes from ______

C Write the base word. The first one has been done for you.

1. filling comes from *fill*
2. helping comes from ______
3. weeding comes from ______
4. feeling comes from ______
5. stealing comes from ______
6. playing comes from ______
7. climbing comes from ______
8. weeping comes from ______

D Write the base word. The first one has been done for you.

1. hoping comes from *hope*
2. riding comes from ______
3. driving comes from ______
4. racing comes from ______
5. liking comes from ______
6. hiking comes from ______
7. skating comes from ______
8. making comes from ______

Parent/Teacher Signature Date

Possessives

To show that someone or something owns something you add an apostrophe and **s** after the word. Example: the bike of the boy = the boy's bike

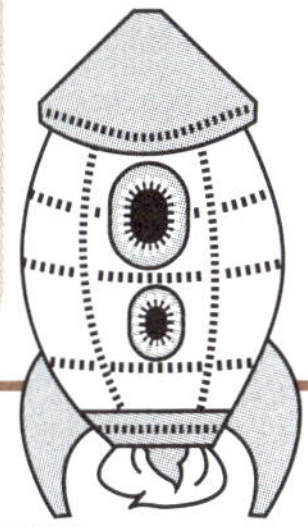

A Make each word show the possessive **s**. The first one has been done for you. Draw a picture for each one.

1. the book of the girl *the girl's book*	**2.** the leaf of the tree __________	**3.** the dress of the lady __________
4. the horns of the cow __________	**5.** the wheels of the car __________	**6.** the pen of the man __________

B Rewrite these phrases to show ownership. The first one has been done for you.

1. the colours of the rainbow *the rainbow's colours*
2. the roof of the house __________
3. the horse of the farmer __________
4. the legs of the piano __________
5. the captain of the team __________
6. the bone of the dog __________
7. the helmet of the worker __________
8. the book of the teacher __________

Parent/Teacher Signature Date

UNIT 50

Revision

A Write the base words for all the words in the box under their headings below.

swimming	skating	hopping	baking
chasing	chopping	hoping	planning

Double last letter + ing **Drop e + ing**

_______ _______ _______ _______

_______ _______ _______ _______

B Make these words end in ing and write them in the spaces.

1. drop ________ 5. dive ________
2. skate ________ 6. slip ________
3. run ________ 7. bite ________
4. gaze ________ 8. skip ________

C Add an apostrophe and an s to show the possessive for these words. The first one has been done for you.

1. the pages of the book *the book's pages*
2. the ink of the pen ________
3. the jumper of the boy ________
4. the blade of the knife ________
5. the shovel of the worker ________
6. the tractor of the farmer ________
7. the sting of the wasp ________
8. the bridle of the horse ________

Parent/Teacher Signature Date

Test

Choose the correct spelling of the words in brackets.
Write the correct words in the spaces.

1 The boy is (swimming, swiming) across the pool. [1]

2 The bird is (flaping, flapping) its wings. [2]

3 Sophie is (diging, digging) a hole. [3]

4 Mia is (mopping, moping) the floor. [4]

5 The children are (danceing, dancing) on the stage. [5]

6 The sailor is (waving, waveing) to me. [6]

7 I am (pasteing, pasting) in the pictures. [7]

8 I am (hopeing, hoping) she arrives soon. [8]

9 Tom (skipped, skiped) across the room. [9]

10 I saw the (boy's, boys) jumper. [10]

11 We looked for our (teachers, teacher's) lost watch. [11]

12 I mended the (books, book's) torn page. [12]

Total correct ______ / 12

Parent/Teacher Signature   Date

UNIT 52

Contractions

Contractions are shortened words. Often we join two words and shorten the second word by leaving out one or more letters. An apostrophe takes the place of the missing letter or letters. Example: you had = you'd

A Choose the right contraction from the box for the words below and write them on the lines.

can't	**it's**	**wasn't**	**isn't**
I'll	**I'm**	**didn't**	**we've**

1. we have ________________
2. it is ________________
3. was not ________________
4. can not ________________
5. did not ________________
6. I will ________________
7. I am ________________
8. is not ________________

B Write the two words for each contraction below.

1. he's ___________ ___________
2. doesn't ___________ ___________
3. what's ___________ ___________
4. they're ___________ ___________
5. we've ___________ ___________
6. he'll ___________ ___________
7. who's ___________ ___________
8. she'll ___________ ___________

C Replace the two words in the brackets with a contraction.

1. He is not sure if (I have) ________________ been invited.
2. I just (can not) ________________ do this.
3. She does not know (what is) ________________ the matter.
4. It (does not) ________________ seem to be getting any better.

Parent/Teacher Signature   Date

Homographs

Some words are spelled the same and are pronounced the same but they have different meanings.
Example: round (shape); round (of golf)

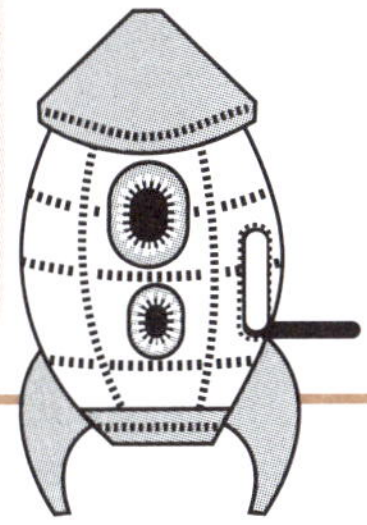

A Use each word in the box twice. Put each in a sentence below.

train	**box**	**bank**	**sink**

1. I put all the toys in the large ________________.
2. Ella deposited fifty dollars in her ________________ account.
3. After they collided the two ships began to ____________ beneath the waves.
4. Some swimmers ________________ every day to get faster.
5. Sam is learning to ________________ so he can protect himself.
6. The boys sat on the ________________ of the river and threw their lines in.
7. After tea we washed the dishes in the ________________.
8. We caught an express ________________ from Melbourne to Sydney.

B Choose the word from the box that has the two meanings below.

match	**post**	**ball**	**jam**
bark	**pen**	**crane**	**bill**

1. an animal enclosure and a writing tool ____________________
2. part of a fence and to mail a letter ____________________
3. a lighting tool and a sporting event ____________________
4. a round object and a formal dance event ____________________
5. something to eat on bread and to get something caught ____________________
6. a duck's beak and the cost of something ____________________
7. sound a dog makes and part of a tree ____________________
8. a bird and a machine used in building ____________________

Parent/Teacher Signature Date

Silent letters

Many words contain silent, or unsounded, letters. In the past some of these letters were sounded and have been left in the word even though today they are silent, as in **calf** and **knee**.

A All the words in the box contain a silent letter. Write each word below and circle the silent letter. Draw a picture for each one.

1. comb	**2. lamb**	**3. thistle**	**4. knee**
5. calf	**6. palm**	**7. knife**	**8. castle**

1. ____________	**2.** ____________	**3.** ____________	**4.** ____________
5. ____________	**6.** ____________	**7.** ____________	**8.** ____________

B The silent letter in brackets is missing from each word. Write the word correctly.

1. (b) crum ________________ (small piece of bread)
2. (b) bom ________________ (explosive)
3. (h) scool ________________ (place of learning)
4. (t) thisle ________________ (prickly bush)
5. (b) lim ________________ (part of the body)
6. (c) sent ________________ (perfume)
7. (l) yok ________________ (part of an egg)
8. (w) sord ________________ (steel weapon)

Parent/Teacher Signature Date

Sound patterns, vowels

Many words have very similar sounds and spellings, sometimes with only one vowel sound that is different.

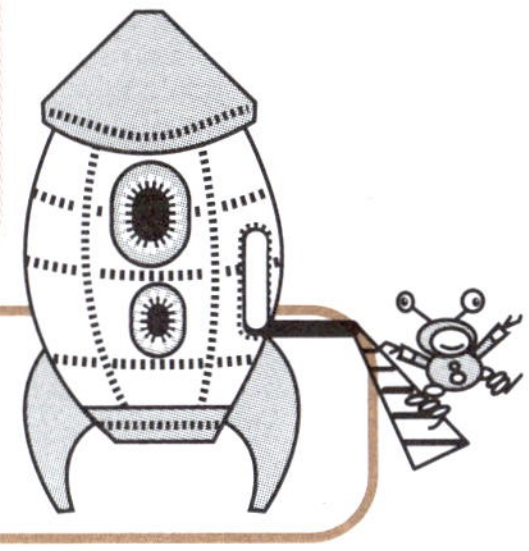

A Change the underlined letter to make a word that matches the definition.

1. bid	you sleep in one	______________
2. like	body of water	______________
3. cap	you drink from it	______________
4. smell	little	______________
5. dock	farmyard bird	______________
6. bell	something that bounces	______________
7. weak	seven days	______________
8. breed	food made from flour	______________

B Change the underlined letter to make a word that matches each picture.

1.  shop ______________	**4.** 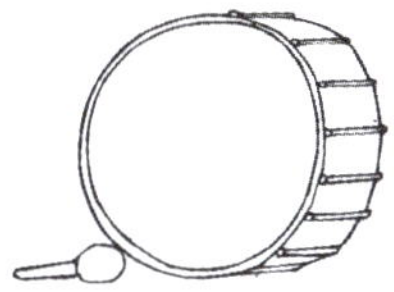 dram ______________	**7.**  bard ______________
2. 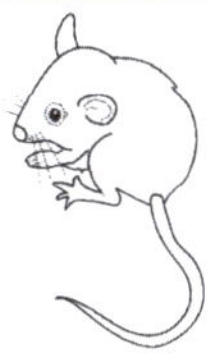 moose ______________	**5.**  sick ______________	**8.**  black ______________
3.  stir ______________	**6.**  hear ______________	**9.**  chain ______________

Parent/Teacher Signature Date

UNIT 56

Hard and soft g and c

A The letter g can be pronounced as a hard g, as in **get** and **gash**, or as a soft g, as in **ginger** and **gypsy**.

Write each word from the box beside its meaning below.

garden	**grape**	**giraffe**	**gem**
gorilla	**goat**	**giant**	**gymnasium**

1. a large ape ____________
2. a room for sports ____________
3. a place where flowers grow ____________
4. a farmyard animal ____________
5. a precious stone ____________
6. something very very large ____________
7. a fruit ____________
8. an animal with a very long neck ____________

B The letter c can be pronounced as a hard c, as in **cat** and **carpet** (a k sound), or it can be a soft c, as in **cell** and **cement** (an s sound).

Write each word from the box under its picture below.

candle	**comet**	**city**	**circle**
cactus	**coffee**	**circus**	**fence**

1.  ______	**2.**  ______	**3.**  ______	**4.**  ______
5.  ______	**6.**  ______	**7.**  ______	**8.**  ______

Parent/Teacher Signature Date

Consonant blends

Consonant blends are groups of two or more letters that are often together, such as dr (dream) and sp (sparrow).

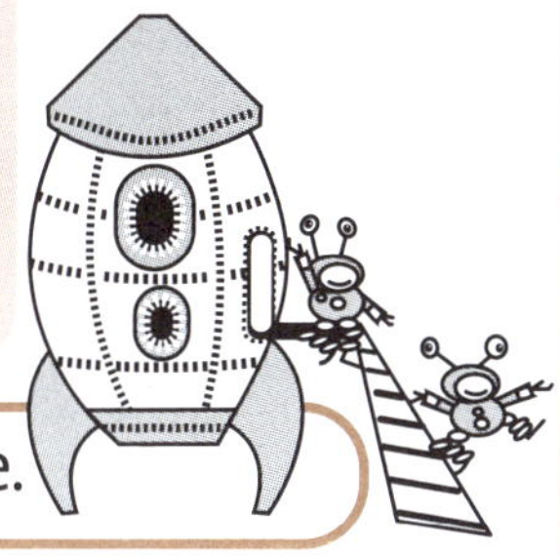

A Write each word from the box in its correct sentence.

blanket
branch
claw
cricket
dream
flower
frozen
grease

1. I like to play ______________ with my friends.
2. During the cold weather the water became ______________.
3. Last night I had a scary ______________ about monsters.
4. It was so cold I put an extra ______________ on my bed.
5. The mechanic smeared some ______________ over the gears of the car.
6. William climbed the tree and stood up on a large ______________.
7. The crab's ______________ snapped in the air.
8. We saw a pretty red ______________ in the garden.

B Add a consonant blend from the box to a word piece below. Draw a picture for each word.

sm	sl	sc	pr
sn	tr	tw	sp

1.	**2.**	**3.**	**4.**
_____ipper	_____ince	_____one	_____ow
5.	**6.**	**7.**	**8.**
_____oke	_____iangle	_____anner	_____enty

Parent/Teacher Signature Date

UNIT 58

Sound patterns, scr, str, spr, shr

Many words are spelled using consonant blends. Some that are very common are the letters scr (scram), str (strap), spr (sprint) and shr (shred).

A Use each word from the box to complete the sentences below.

scratch	sprain	shrink	strict
straw	shrub	spring	scribble

1. The farmer spread the ________________ to make a bed for the horse.
2. My little sister did a lot of ________________ in my notebook.
3. Our teacher is ________________ but always fair.
4. The cat began to ________________ the person who held it.
5. A small ________________ with yellow flowers grew on the lawn.
6. Sometimes when you wash clothes they will ________________.
7. Noah must be careful not to ________________ his leg playing sport now.
8. In ________________ the weather usually begins to warm up.

B The words in the box have been cramped up. Find and write each word beside its meaning below.

shrimpshrinestraightstreetsprintspreadscrubscream

1. not bent ________________
2. road with houses along it ____________
3. small water creature ______________
4. short race ________________
5. low trees in the bush ________________
6. sacred place ________________
7. to yell loudly ________________
8. to put things around ________________

Parent/Teacher Signature Date

Sound patterns, ch, sh, ch, th, sq

Some consonants form a new sound when they are together.

A The letters ch together are sounded as in **chat**. The letters sh together are sounded as in **shut**. The letters ck together are sounded as in **rock** (the c is silent). The words in the box have been cramped up. Find each word and write it beside its meaning below.

peachshovelcheesefishbucketchickshampoocricket

1. a container for water ____________
2. water animal with fins ____________
3. a food made from milk ____________
4. a sport ____________
5. a baby bird ____________
6. a fruit ____________
7. a tool for digging ____________
8. soap to wash hair ____________

B The letters th together are often sounded as in **thank**. The letters sq (which are always followed by the vowel u) are sounded as in **square**. Write each word from the box in its correct sentence below.

squeak
square
squirrel
throat
throne
squirt
three

1. The king sat on his ____________.
2. Sophie had a sore ____________ from yelling so much.
3. A lion will roar but a mouse will ____________.
4. He used a water pistol to ____________ water at his friends.
5. A triangle has ____________ sides.
6. A ____________ has four sides.
7. The ____________ hid the nuts it collected in the hollow of the tree.

Parent/Teacher Signature

Date

Syllables

A syllable is a group of letters that has one sounded vowel. Sometimes the first syllable is stressed, so you say that syllable a little louder, and sometimes the last syllable is stressed.
Examples: <u>mar</u> / ket (market); pa / <u>rade</u> (parade)

A Each word below has two syllables. Draw a line to divide the two syllables and underline the stressed syllable. Draw a picture for each one.

1.	2.	3.	4.
carpet	rabbit	pedal	camel
5.	**6.**	**7.**	**8.**
petal	bucket	pencil	shovel

B Use each word from the box to complete the sentences below.

al	**el**	**le**	**et**
ile	**net**	**il**	**it**

1. The workers laid some grav_______ on the road.
2. I lost a sand_______ when I took it off at the park.
3. Oliver pulled the buck_______ on his belt tight.
4. The worker wore a helm_______ on her head.
5. The new satellite will orb_______ around the Earth.
6. Be careful as this thin glass is frag_______ .
7. This mag_______ will attract pieces of steel.
8. The scientist found a foss_______ of a dinosaur.

Parent/Teacher Signature Date

Revision

A Write the words from the box under their correct headings below.

knife	knee	hour	thumb
castle	school	plumber	thistle

Silent k	Silent b	Silent t	Silent h
______	______	______	______
______	______	______	______

B Write the words from the box under their correct headings below.

ground	gypsy	ginger	gate
genie	guard	green	giraffe

Hard g		Soft g	
______	______	______	______
______	______	______	______

C Write the words from the box under their correct headings below.

cousin	climb	cement	cabbage
city	cigar	camel	cell

Hard c		Soft c	
______	______	______	______
______	______	______	______

Parent/Teacher Signature Date

Test 1

The underlined words are spelled wrongly. Write them correctly in the spaces.

	Sentence	Answer
1	He neatened his hair with a brush and com.	1
2	When he walked in the bush a thisle scratched his leg.	2
3	Our teacher is very strickt sometimes.	3
4	We decided to spred the butter on the bread.	4
5	The jiant chased Jack down the beanstalk.	5
6	We are going to the sircus tomorrow.	6
7	I took my new criket bat to school today.	7
8	Charlotte showed me her damaged sliper.	8
9	We made some chease from the milk.	9
10	The boy tried to squert me with a water pistol.	10
11	I filled the buket with water.	11
12	The worker wore a helmit.	12

Total correct ______ / 12

Parent/Teacher Signature Date

Test 2

Choose the correct spelling of the word and write it in the space.

1	The mother sheep protected its (lam, lamb).	1
2	I go to (school, skool) every day.	2
3	The baby did a lot of (skribble, scribble) in the book.	3
4	The farmer fed the (straw, stror) to the cows.	4
5	We saw a (jiraffe, giraffe) at the zoo.	5
6	A (cactus, caktus) is growing in the garden.	6
7	The water in the refrigerator is (frozin, frozen).	7
8	She tightened the nut with a (spanner, spaner).	8
9	Lily drew a (sqare, square) in her book.	9
10	The (chick, chik) stayed close to the old hens.	10
11	He used a (pensil, pencil) to draw a picture.	11
12	I used a (shovil, shovel) to dig a hole.	12

Total correct ______
12

Parent/Teacher Signature Date

UNIT 64

Comparisons

To show comparison between two things we add er to the word. Example: This gum tree is old, but this pine is older.

A Make the underlined words end in er so they fit the meaning of each sentence. The first one has been done for you.

1. Today is cold but yesterday was ___colder___.
2. This sum is hard but that one is ________________.
3. Tom is short but his brother is ________________.
4. Joel is sick but Sophie is ________________.
5. This pie is warm but that one is ________________.
6. Brodie is fast but Sara is ________________.
7. That pool is deep but this one is ________________.
8. This feather is soft but these are ________________.

B Write the correct word in the spaces below and draw a picture for each one.

1.	2.	3.
Mia is tall but Josh is ________________.	An ant is slow but a snail is ________________.	Chloe is neat but Tom is ________________.
4.	**5.**	**6.**
A mouse is small but an ant is ________________.	This string is long but that one is ________________.	This knife is sharp but the big one is ____________.

Parent/Teacher Signature   Date

Prefixes

Prefixes are groups of letters we add to the beginning of a base word.

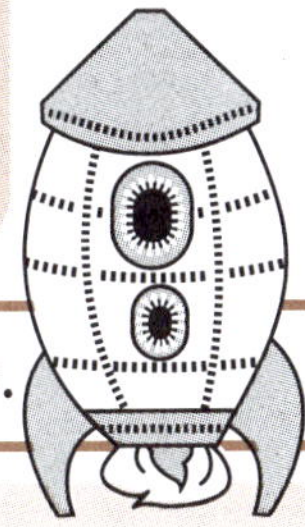

A Choose a prefix from the box to complete the words.

post **sub** **ex** **in**

1. When it went behind the cloud the plane was ______visible.
2. We were worried that the bomb might ______plode.
3. We travelled in the ______way.
4. Because it is so wet we will have to ______pone the match.

B Choose a prefix from the list to complete the words to match the pictures.

mis **non** **bi** **sub** **tri** **un**

1. 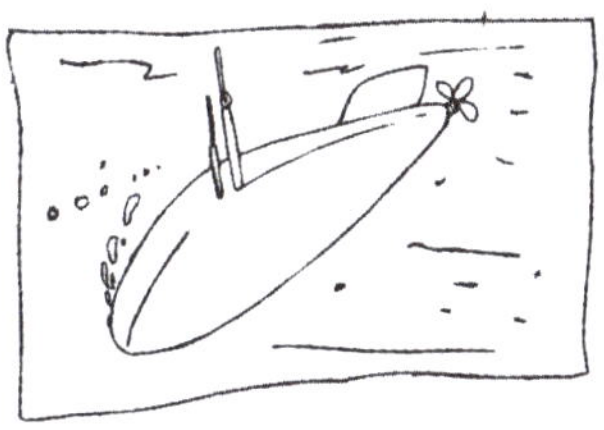 ______marine	**2.**  ______cycle	**3.**  ______smoking
4.  ______take	**5.** 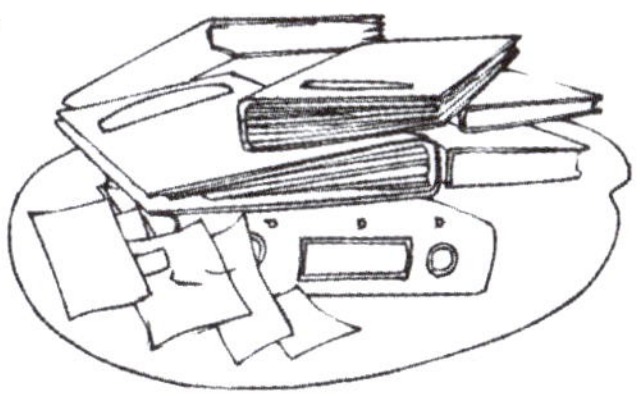 ______tidy	**6.**  ______angle

Parent/Teacher Signature Date

Suffixes

Suffixes are groups of letters we add to the end of a base word.
Example: use + less = useless; safe + ly = safely

A Add a suffix from the box to complete the words below to make each one fit the meaning of the sentence.

ous	ion	ly	able
ive	ary	ful	ish

1. The sun was shining bright_____ through the clouds.
2. We had a very enjoy_____ day at the picnic.
3. Our year took up a collect_____ of money for the poor people.
4. Be careful because this snake is very poison_____.
5. The shoes we bought were very expens_____.
6. You must be care_____ when you cross a busy road.
7. That boy is very fool_____.
8. We read the new books in the libr_____.

B Add the correct suffix to complete each word. Use a dictionary if you need to.

1. The long run made me breath________. (less, liss)
2. Sarah's new outfit is very styl______. (ich, ish)
3. The train pulled into the sta______. (tion, sion)
4. The boys' behaviour can be very tire______. (some, sum)
5. The old bridge is quite danger______. (ous, ius)
6. Tom's brother is a guitar______ (est, ist)
7. The attend______ looked after our luggage. (ent, ant)
8. Mum grows lots of ed______ plants in her garden. (able, ible)

Parent/Teacher Signature Date

Word endings

Many word endings use letter patterns but some letter patterns are very similar so it is easy to confuse them. Examples: baker and actor

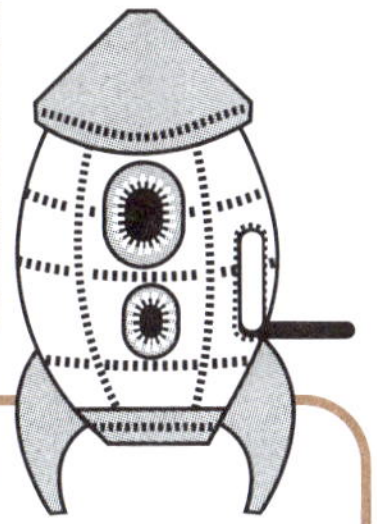

A Choose the correct group of letters to complete each word. Draw a picture for each one.

1.	**2.**	**3.**
apr______ (on, an)	chick______ (in, en)	fount_______ (ian, ain)
4.	**5.**	**6.**
turk_______ (ey, ay)	dais_______ (y, i)	tenn_______ (us, is)

B Add the correct ending from the box to complete the words in the sentences below.

or	**en**	**ain**	**y**
er	**ar**	**ey**	**age**

1. The glass was brok______ when it fell on the floor.
2. We climbed all the way up the mount______.
3. The farmer used his tract______ to plough the paddock.
4. I ate the sweet berr______ I picked from the tree.
5. At the supermarket I pushed a troll______ around.
6. The traveller put her lugg______ on the train.
7. I spent the doll______ coin I was given.
8. My moth______ works at a garage.

Parent/Teacher Signature   Date

UNIT 68

Revision

A Complete the words in the box and write them under their headings below.

teach_____	**kitt_____**	**gard_____**	**tract_____**
doll_____	**act_____**	**sug_____**	**scoot_____**
doct_____	**coll_____**	**mot_____**	**cell_____**
childr_____	**powd_____**	**rubb_____**	**chick_____**

+ or	**+ er**	**+ ar**	**+ en**
__________	__________	__________	__________
__________	__________	__________	__________
__________	__________	__________	__________
__________	__________	__________	__________

B Choose the correct prefix for each word to match the picture.

1.  ______cycle (bi, mis)	**2.**  ______riangle (tri, qud)	**3.** 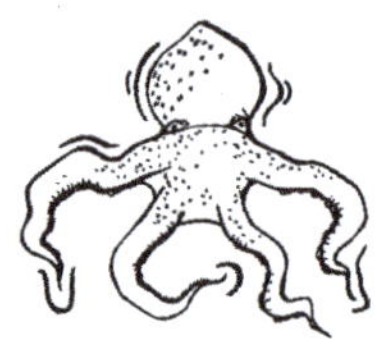 ______pus (octo, duo)
4. 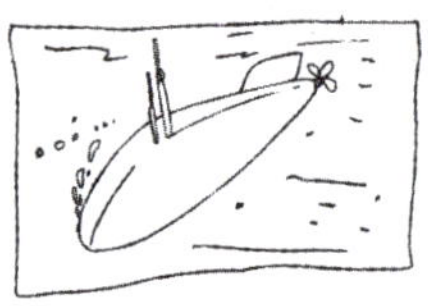 ______marine (sub, ex)	**5.**  ______plosion (ex, en)	**6.**  ______head (fore, dis)

Parent/Teacher Signature Date

Test

The underlined words are spelled wrongly. Write the correct spellings in the spaces.

	Sentence	Answer
1	Today is warm but yesterday was warmar.	1
2	This rope is shorta than that one.	2
3	I rode a bycycle to school.	3
4	She drew a tryangle in her book.	4
5	I'm afraid these books are usles to us.	5
6	I read an interesting book in the libary.	6
7	I caught the train at the railway stashun.	7
8	I like to play tennas.	8
9	The glass was brokin when it fell.	9
10	My mothar is taking us to the circus.	10
11	Our teachir comes from Darwin.	11
12	There is a large fountin in the city square.	12

Total correct ______ / 12

Parent/Teacher Signature   Date

UNIT 70

Anagrams 1

Anagrams are words that have exactly the same letters but in a different order. Example: post, spot

A Rearrange the letters of these words and draw a picture for each one.

1.	**2.**	**3.**	**4.**
sub ________	pat ________	ramp ________	tan ________
5.	**6.**	**7.**	**8.**
flow ________	ails ________	east ________	grin ________

B Rearrange the words in brackets to make new words to complete each sentence.

1. We went for a swim in the ______________. (loop)
2. I poured the cereal into the ______________. (blow)
3. Sophie came first and Cooper came ______________ in the race. (salt)
4. I really ______________ a lot for my puppy. (race)
5. We saw a ______________ twinkling. (rats)
6. The large ______________ stung him. (paws)
7. He could not find the ______________ he had lost. (hose)
8. The ______________ on the grass sparkled. (wed)

Parent/Teacher Signature Date

Anagrams 2

Anagrams are words that have exactly the same letters but in a different order. Example: post, spot

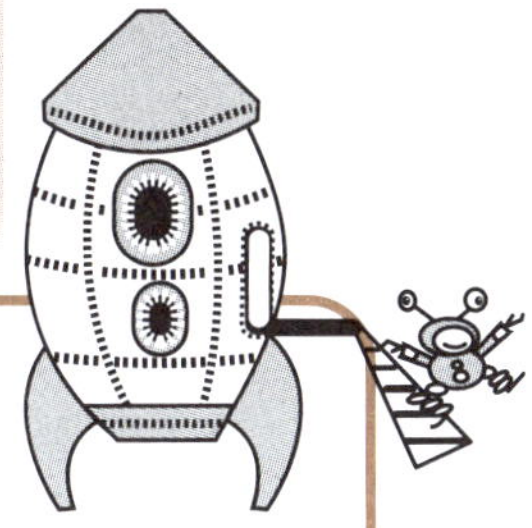

A Rearrange the letters of each word in the box to make a new word. Use the new word to complete each sentence below.

sore	**pea**	**tame**	**post**
grin	**ate**	**edit**	**lair**

1. She wore a gold ______________ on her finger.
2. The driver decided to ______________ at the corner.
3. Sometimes I think Will is a ______________ as he tells untruths all the time.
4. We waited for the ______________ to come in before going for a swim.
5. I had a cup of ______________ with my meal.
6. A gorilla is a large ______________ of Africa.
7. I picked a beautiful red ______________ from the garden.
8. I play in the same football ______________ as my brother.

B Rearrange the letters of each word in the box and write it in the space. Draw a picture for each one.

1. east	**2. rats**	**3. lump**	**4. reap**
5. save	**6. palm**	**7. low**	**8. pore**

1. ______________	**2.** ______________	**3.** ______________	**4.** ______________
5. ______________	**6.** ______________	**7.** ______________	**8.** ______________

Parent/Teacher Signature Date

Changing words

The meaning of some words has changed over hundreds of years. For example, the word **nice** originally meant **stupid**. You can change a word's meaning by changing just one letter.

Change the first letter of each word below to make a word that matches the definition. Draw a picture for each one.

1. heard (hair on the chin)	**6.** park (noise of a dog)	**11.** bony (small horse)
2. house (small animal)	**7.** dish (water creature)	**12.** reach (seaside)
3. come (where you live)	**8.** gorse (riding animal)	**13.** bear (fruit)
4. leather (birds have them)	**9.** honey (you spend it)	**14.** dairy (magical person)
5. golf (dog-like animal)	**10.** guppy (baby dog)	**15.** grange (citrus fruit)

Parent/Teacher Signature Date

Review

A Write the words from the box under their headings below

apple	pony	splash	cake
frog	teeth	finger	wept
spider	swift	hive	stop
woke	cent	snake	here

Long a sound	Short a sound	Long e sound	Short e sound
______	______	______	______
______	______	______	______

Long i sound	Short i sound	Long o sound	Short o sound
______	______	______	______
______	______	______	______

B Make the plural of each word in the box and write them under their headings below

egg	box	tray
fly	house	story
bus	lolly	pony
catch	monkey	bush

+ s	+ es	Change y to i + es
______	______	______
______	______	______
______	______	______
______	______	______

Parent/Teacher Signature Date

Test 1

Choose the correct spelling from the words in the brackets. Write the correct words in the spaces.

1 I saw a (whale, wale) at the beach. [1]

2 There is a football (mach, match) on today. [2]

3 I found the jobs (eesy, easy) to do. [3]

4 We went on a (piknic, picnic) yesterday. [4]

5 Ella took three (caches, catches). [5]

6 Sophie has lots of (dreses, dresses). [6]

7 There were lots of (foxs, foxes) in the forest. [7]

8 My little brother has lots of (tois, toys) to play with. [8]

9 I saw three (donkies, donkeys) at the farm. [9]

10 Do you like to play (futball, football)? [10]

11 I like to eat (strawberries, strorberries). [11]

12 I fell asleep in the (armchare, armchair). [12]

Total correct ______ / 12

Parent/Teacher Signature Date

Test 2

The underlined words are spelled incorrectly. Write the correct spelling of each word in the space.

1	When he fell he hurt his big <u>towe</u>.	1
2	We have a large <u>clok</u> in our room.	2
3	I like to listen to <u>mousic</u>.	3
4	We walked <u>unda</u> the arch.	4
5	I heard the dog <u>barck</u>.	5
6	The colour of this flower is <u>perple</u>.	6
7	I filled the <u>bottel</u> with water.	7
8	The <u>docta</u> listened to my heart beat.	8
9	I <u>pinnd</u> the chart on the wall.	9
10	Lachlan <u>draged</u> the bin across the yard.	10
11	Riley is <u>kiking</u> the football.	11
12	Jack <u>droped</u> the glass.	12

Total correct ______ / 12

Parent/Teacher Signature　　　　Date

UNIT 76

Test 3

Choose the correct spelling from the words in brackets and write it in the space.

1	Noah (war, wore, whorre) a new shirt today.	1
2	I read a (verse, virs, vers) of a poem.	2
3	I (hurd, heard, herd) a funny noise.	3
4	Today is the (frist, ferst, first) day of the week.	4
5	At the farm we saw a (goose, guse, goos).	5
6	I ate tomato (supe, soop, soup) for lunch.	6
7	Our (howse, house, huse) has a red roof.	7
8	We are (hoping, hopeing, hopen) he will come.	8
9	Tom is (driveng, dryving, driving) his dad's car.	9
10	We are (chopping, chopen, choping) up the wood.	10
11	Mia is (swiming, swimming, swimmen) across the pool.	11
12	I cut the meat with a (nife, knife, knyve).	12

Total correct ______ / 12

Parent/Teacher Signature

Date

Useful Words

able
above
across
afternoon
age
air
along
any
anything
around
band
bear
became
become
began
belong
better
black
boat
bound
brother
burn
buy
camp
cannot
car
care
cent
city
class
clean

clear
clothing
club
coming
cost
could
cover
cure
dark
dash
delay
down
east
easy
even
every
express
eye
fail
father
fell
felt
fight
fill
fine
finish
fire
first
found
Friday
from

full
game
girl
glad
glass
gold
gone
grand
grant
half
hard
head
help
here
high
hill
hope
horse
hour
hurt
July
June
keep
kind
lady
large
left
lesson
life
light
line

lost
made
magic mail
may
maybe
mile
mine
more
most
move
name
near
never
news
night
only
open
our
outside
part
partly
party
pass
pay
place
poor
price
print
race
rain
reach

read
report
rest
right
room
round
said
same
saw
seam
seem
sent
set
ship
short
should
shut
side
sir
small
soap
son
spell
stamp
state
step
still
story
suit
summer
table

talk
tent
they
tonight
track
train
try
turn
two
under
unless
upon
walk
want
war
warm
watch
water
weak
week
when
where
why
wife
wind
with
without
word
work
would

WINK: Words I Need to Know

For many people, some words are often problematic to spell. Record words you are having difficulty with on this page.

Word	Word	Word

Some Tips for Learning to Spell

★ When you read, look out for the patterns of letters you find in words. Remembering these will help you spell words. For example, these words do not sound the same, but all contain a common letter pattern: cough, rough, through, thought, bough.

★ Take an interest in words, as this is useful in motivating you to persevere with improving your spelling ability.

★ Accept that some difficult words simply have to be learned. A useful strategy for this is the LOOK, COVER, WRITE, CHECK system.

> LOOK at the word and try to form a pattern of the letters in your mind. Ensure you know the meaning of the word and how it is used.
>
> COVER the word or remove it from your sight.
>
> WRITE the word from memory.
>
> CHECK if you are correct.

If wrong, begin the process again. If right, give yourself a pat on the back.

★ Learn to say words correctly. Many students often have spelling difficulties simply because they pronounce some words incorrectly, and spell them as they think they sound. For example: jumping, not jumpen.

★ Develop the dictionary habit. If you don't know how to spell a word, look it up. Did you know a dictionary is used more for finding the correct spelling of words rather than finding their meanings?

★ Become familiar with the more common rules and guides, and use them.

★ When you are writing and you have guessed the spelling of a word, always check it later.

★ Remember that incorrect spelling is easily noticed by others, so being a good speller can be an aid to employment.

Assessment

	T1	T2	T3	T4
★ Reads widely and takes an interest in words and their meanings.				
★ Is prepared to make informed attempts at spelling.				
★ Spells at a standard commensurate with his or her age.				
★ Uses a variety of methods to improve spelling skills, such as sounds and patterns.				
★ Takes care to review and proofread own writing attempts.				
★ Readily identifies errors in proofreading activities.				
★ Continually displays a determination and desire to improve spelling.				
★ Is aware that words that sound the same may have different spellings.				
★ Makes correct vowel alternation from long to short vowels.				

Comments

Teacher

____

____

Student

____

____

Glossary of Terms

adjective
A word that describes nouns or other words.
Examples: **gold** (noun), **golden** (adjective)
wool (noun), **woollen** (adjective)

anagram
The letters of a *word* or words that can make another word when jumbled up.
Example: **fowl** and **wolf**

base word
A *word* to which *prefixes* and *suffixes* can be added.
Example: obey (base word) + **dis** (prefix) = disobey + **ed** (suffix) = disobeyed

comparative
An *adjective* that shows degrees of comparison.
Examples: fat (one), fatter (two), fattest (three or more); Jack is tall but Tom is taller.

compound word
A *word* made up of two or more smaller words, often developing first as a hyphenated word.
Example: **butter** + **fly** = **butterfly**.

consonant
A letter in which the air is in some way impeded when pronounced. There are 21 consonants in the alphabet, all the letters that are not *vowels*.

consonant blend
When two or more *consonants* come together to blend a sound. Examples: **stick**, **sky**, **brown**, **straw**
Consonant blends may be initial blends (**frog**), medial (middle) blends (**blister**), or final blends (**stamp**).

contraction
A *word* in which one or more letters have been omitted and in their place an apostrophe inserted.
Examples: **I would** becomes **I'd**; **is not** becomes **isn't**

digraph
A combination of letters that represents a single sound. There are *consonant* digraphs and *vowel* digraphs. Common consonant digraphs include **sh**, **ch**, **th** and **wh**. (Consonant digraphs at the beginning of a word are called an onset; vowel digraphs are also called diphthongs.)

homograph
A *word* that is spelled the same as another word, but each word is pronounced differently and has a different meaning (a type of *homonym*). Examples: **desert** (dry barren area) and **desert** (abandon); **close** (near) and **close** (shut)

homonym
A *word* that is spelled and/or pronounced the same as another word but each word has a different meaning. *Homographs* and *homophones* are both types of homonym, and some homonyms are both homographs and homophones. Examples: **tear** (rip) and **tear** (result of crying); **fair** (blond) and **fare** (cost of a train ticket); **bank** (place to exchange money) and **bank** (either side of a river)

homophone
A *word* that is pronounced the same as another word, but each word has a different spelling and a different meaning (a type of *homonym*). Examples: **bear** (a furry animal) and **bare** (naked); **sure** (certain) and **shore** (coastline)

letter pattern
A letter sequence that functions as a unit and is related to a consistent category of sound.
Example: **one** = **bone**, **cone**, **tone**

long vowel
The sound of a *vowel* (**a**, **e**, **i**, **o**, **u**) that says its letter name, or is an **r**-*influenced vowel.*
Examples: **same**, **bacon**, **far**, **concrete**, **fever**, **fine**, **rival**, **fir**, **cone**, **robot**, **core**, **cute**, **student**, **purr**

noun
A *word* that refers to the names of everything around us.

phonics
The systematic relationship between letters and sounds.

plural
More than one. Most words make their plurals by adding an s. However, there are other ways to make the plurals of words. Examples: **girl**, **girls**; **watch**, **watches**; **city**, **cities**; **piano**, **pianos**; **knife**, **knives**; **tooth**, **teeth**; **mouse**, **mice**

possessive
A *word* that uses an apostrophe to show that someone (or something) has ownership.
Examples: the boy's bike; the ladies' dresses

prefix
Letters added to the beginning of a *word*, sometimes to make its opposite. We simply add these and no spelling changes to the base word are necessary.
Example: in + visible = **invisible**

r-influenced vowel
A *vowel* sound that is determined by the letter r following it. Example: The a in **far** is a *long vowel* sound but the a in **fad** is a *short vowel* sound.

root word
A *word* or word part that has its origin in Old English, Latin or Greek and that provides the basis of many other words. Example: aero (air) = **aerial**, **aeroplane**, **aerobics**

short vowel
The sound of a *vowel* (a, e, i, o and u) that is clipped — a short sound. It is sometimes said short vowel sounds are the "baby" sounds.
Examples: **bat**, **bet**, **bit**, **bottle**, **but**

silent (unsounded) letter
A letter in some words that is not pronounced but is still included in the word. Examples: **lamb**, **know**, **pneumonia**, **sword**, **wrap**

suffix
A *word* ending that alters the word's part of speech (noun to adjective, for example) or meaning. Spelling changes are often needed.
Example: **beauty** + ful = **beautiful**

syllable
A sound unit that includes only one sounded *vowel*. The vowel may be preceded or followed by several *consonants*. Words can be divided into their syllables. This is a useful spelling technique.
Example: **development** = de / vel / op / ment

vowel
A letter in which the air passes through the mouth without obstruction when pronounced. The letters a, e, i, o and u are vowels. Note: y does the work of the vowels i and e in words such as **cry** (long i), **mystery** (short i) and **weary** (long e).

word
A unit of meaning. A word may be a simple syllable or a combination of syllables. A word may contain smaller units of meaning with it.

word history
The study of how *words* have developed over the years to become part of our modern everyday language.

Answers, Class 3

Unit 1

A

1.waiter
2. daisy
3. plate
4. safety
5. tame
6. snake
7. baby
8. sailor

B

1. whale
2. hate
3. stable
4. rake
5. cage
6. brave
7. face
8. plane

Unit 2

A

1. hammer
2. apple
3. ladder
4. magic
5. shadow
6. cactus
7. tadpole
8. sand

B

1. splash
2. match
3. catch
4. camel
5. wagon
6. batter
7. happen
8. fancy

Unit 3

A

1. sheep
2. queen
3. these
4. evening
5. squeak
6. creek
7. niece
8. wheel
9. freeze

B

1. weak
2. teeth
3. steam
4. here
5. sweet
6. scene
7. dream
8. fleas

Unit 4

A

1. wept
2. cent
3. drench
4. eggs
5. left
6. tennis
7. bread
8. dead

B

1. melt
2. desk
3. left
4. sketch
5. lead
6. shelf
7. fresh
8. swept

Unit 5

A

1. pilot
2. hive
3. crime
4. pirate
5. white
6. spider
7. knife
8. pile

B

1. smile
2. wise
3. alive
4. tighten
5. silent
6. higher
7. like
8. bright

C

1. hive
2. tiger
3. bike
4. spider

Unit 6

A

1. picnic
2. winter
3. swift
4. fifty
5. river
6. sister
7. hiss
8. visit

B

1. chimney
2. finger
3. pillow
4. mitten
5. dinner
6. kitten
7. slipper
8. window

Unit 7 Revision

A

Long a:
tame
snake
plate
baby
Short a:
apple
hammer
tadpole
splash

B

Long e:
here
scene
sheep
squeak
Short e:
desk
sketch
dead
fresh

C

Long i:
crime
icy
spice
high
Short i:
finger
fist
kitten
sister

Unit 8 Test 1

1. baby
2. snake
3. apple
4. face
5. freeze
6. weak
7. bread
8. sketch
9. spider
10. silent
11. winter
12. city

Unit 9 Test 2

1. waiter
2. whale
3. hammer
4. happen
5. niece
6. dream
7. wept
8. cent
9. white
10. tighten
11. river
12. visit

Unit 10

A

1. trees
2. tables
3. flowers
4. birds

B
1. bottles
2. girls
3. books
4. cakes
5. computers
6. supermarkets
7. lights
8. hats

Unit 11
A
1. peaches
2. dishes
3. bushes
4. churches
B
1. catches
2. stitches
3. wishes
4. bushes
5. crashes
6. watches
7. matches
8. witches

Unit 12
A
1. buses
2. foxes
3. boxes
4. dresses
B
1. gases
2. dresses
3. glasses
4. guesses
5. faxes
6. bosses
7. buzzes
8. passes

Unit 13
A
1. trays
2. monkeys
3. keys
4. toys
B
1. holidays
2. donkeys
3. boys
4. trolleys
5. kidneys
6. days
7. jockeys
8. turkeys

Unit 14 Revision
A
+ s:
pens
turkeys
coins
trays
toys
birds
+ es:
gases
boxes
beaches
dishes
bushes
guesses
B
1. boys
2. jockeys
3. brushes
4. pets
5. matches
6. branches
7. peaches
8. dresses
C
1. donkeys
2. beaches
3. apples
4. buses

Unit 15 Test
1. pencils
2. shops
3. bushes
4. buses
5. dresses
6. monkeys
7. donkeys
8. keys
9. glasses
10. cats
11. ways
12. wishes

Unit 16
A
1. starfish
2. carport
3. waterfall
4. grasshopper
5. toothbrush
6. strawberry
7. footpath
8. windmill
B
1. bulldog
2. tugboat
3. football
4. seaside
5. jellyfish
6. overcoat
7. campfire
8. homework

Unit 17
A
1. mailbox
2. toothpaste
3. armchair
4. baseball
5. crossroads
6. whiteboard
7. backyard
8. necklace
B
1. freeway
2. basketball
3. tablecloth
4. eggcup
5. butterfly
6. matchbox
7. horseshoe
8. haystack

Unit 18
A
Vegetables:
carrot
bean
cabbage
lettuce
Fruit:
cherry
grape
apple
peach
Cereal grains:
rice
wheat
oats
barley
B
Shapes:
triangle
square
rectangle
oblong
Sports:
tennis
badminton
football
cricket
Vehicles:
car
truck
van
motorbike
C
Space:
star
rocket
comet
planet
Garden:
seeds
hose
hoe
flowers
Home:
bathroom
carpet
sink
cupboard

Unit 19
A
1. toes
2. pony
3. rose
4. bones
5. doze
6. close
7. frozen
8. nose
B
1. broken
2. donate
3. homework

4. hopeful
5. postage
6. toaster
7. mower
8. lonely

C

1. sofa
2. ocean
3. rope
4. motor

Unit 20

1. dollar
2. pocket
3. knob
4. frog
5. golf
6. soft
7. clock
8. stop

B

1. shop
2. pond
3. lost
4. moth
5. lock
6. bottle
7. doctor
8. crop

C

1. shot
2. long

Unit 21

1. tune
2. student
3. fumes
4. cute
5. tulip
6. huge
7. music
8. tube

B

1. bugle
2. mule
3. perfume
4. cube
5. cure
6. beauty
7. rescue
8. picture

Unit 22

A

1. funnel
2. button
3. butterfly
4. umpire
5. puppy
6. bucket
7. tunnel
8. drum

B

1. plug
2. crust
3. supper
4. puzzle
5. buzz
6. number
7. ugly
8. under

Unit 23

1. card
2. cart
3. shark
4. park
5. jar
6. star
7. garden
8. harp

B

1. spark
2. sharp
3. large
4. target
5. artist
6. march
7. bark
8. dark

Unit 24

A

1. purr
2. hurt
3. spur
4. burn
5. church
6. surf
7. return
8. hurl

B

1. burst
2. nurse
3. purple
4. purse
5. burned
6. curtain
7. curl
8. curb

Unit 25 Revision

A

Long o:
bone
sofa
rope
postage
Short o:
moth
pocket
frog
clock

B

Long u:
tulip
huge
pure
tune
Short u:
button
thunder
butter
umpire

C

ar:
farm
scar
harm
cart
ur:
purr
church
burst
hurt

Unit 26 Test 1

1. rose
2. toaster
3. bottle
4. pocket
5. music
6. perfume
7. butter
8. puzzle
9. star
10. target
11. return
12. curtain

Unit 27 Test 2

1. bone
2. homework
3. clock
4. doctor
5. tune
6. rescue
7. bucket
8. supper
9. start
10. dark
11. burn
12. burst

Unit 28

A

1. flies
2. ladies
3. ponies
4. poppies

B

1. cities
2. stories
3. berries
4. libraries
5. diaries
6. hobbies
7. babies
8. jellies

Unit 29

A

1. asked
2. played
3. showed
4. cooked

B

1. landed
2. looked
3. rushed
4. ended
5. milked
6. backed
7. camped
8. planted

Unit 30

A

1. wishing
2. dressing
3. hatching
4. kicking
5. flying
6. singing

B

1. fishing
2. washing
3. lifting
4. licking
5. eating
6. reading

Unit 31

A

1. chopped
2. patted
3. dropped
4. rubbed

B

1. stopping
2. clapping
3. dragging
4. planning
5. shopping
6. skipping
7. mopping
8. hopping

Unit 32 Revision

A

+ s:
boys
toys
holidays
monkeys
donkeys
keys
Change y to i + es:
babies
cities
flies
stories
armies
poppies

B

+ ed:
played
fished
shocked
asked
camped
rushed
Double last letter + ed:
stopped
scrubbed
rubbed
clapped
mopped
planned

C

1. planting
2. wishing
3. dropping
4. mopping

Unit 33 Test

1. blowflies
2. berries
3. jellies
4. stories
5. looked
6. camped
7. milked
8. chopped
9. dragged
10. rubbed
11. lifting
12. reading

Unit 34

A

1. pear
2. bean
3. ball
4. eight
5. sea
6. tow
7. flower
8. rose

B

1. steal
2. fir
3. week
4. weak
5. deer
6. steel
7. fur
8. dear

Unit 35

A

1. rain
2. one
3. mail
4. toe
5. pear
6. see
7. flower
8. sun

B

1. tale, tail
2. whole, hole
3. creak, creek
4. rode, road
5. stair, stare
6. knew, new

C

1. plane
2. rose
3. bean
4. wood

Unit 36

1. aquarium
2. bicycle
3. asteroid
4. television
5. graph
6. thermometer
7. dentist
8. pedestrian

Unit 37

A

1. short
2. horse
3. shore
4. course
5. torch
6. storm
7. north
8. before

B

1. corn
2. pork
3. wore
4. pour
5. roar
6. cork

Unit 38

A

1. verse
2. deer
3. learn
4. cheer
5. spear
6. fern
7. year
8. perch

B

1. herbs
2. swerve
3. heart
4. steer
5. beard
6. hear
7. beer
8. term

Unit 39

A

1. circus
2. first
3. wire
4. skirt
5. squirt
6. spire
7. shirt
8. girl

B

1. thirty
2. stir
3. circus
4. dirty
5. shirt
6. dirt
7. wire
8. hire

Unit 40

A

1. gown
2. towel
3. flowers
4. clown
5. crowd
6. shower
7. crown
8. tower

B

1. mower
2. pillow
3. snow
4. window
5. elbow
6. rowing
7. shadow
8. throwing

Unit 41

A

1. noose
2. goose
3. rooster
4. cocoon
5. stool
6. hoop
7. snooze
8. broom

B

1. cooking
2. took
3. book
4. wooden
5. shook
6. wool
7. hood
8. foot

Unit 42

A

1. coat
2. toad
3. toast
4. boat
5. goat
6. soap
7. float
8. loaf

B

1. flour
2. pouch
3. crouch
4. soup
5. cousin
6. found
7. south
8. shout

Unit 43 Revision

A

or:
store
north
corn
horse

er:
verse
germ
term
fern

B

ir:
bird
first
squirt
girl

ow:
mower
pillow
flower
snow

C

long oo:
goose
rooster
stool
snooze

short oo:
foot
wood
cook
hood

Unit 44 Test 1

1. shore
2. horse
3. fern
4. heart
5. bird
6. circus
7. flower
8. tower
9. loose
10. wooden
11. soap
12. pouch

Unit 45 Test 2

1. storm
2. roar
3. verse
4. wear
5. thirsty
6. stir
7. crown
8. mower
9. goose
10. cooking
11. float
12. soup

Unit 46

A

1. grated
2. divided
3. lined
4. dared
5. loved
6. hoped

B

1. faced
2. exploded
3. liked
4. eroded
5. lied
6. dived
7. raved
8. fined

Unit 47

A

1. chasing
2. racing
3. baking
4. dancing
5. waving
6. driving

B

1. taming
2. wasting
3. grazing
4. blazing
5. pasting
6. using

Unit 48

A

1. watch
2. kick
3. knock
4. waste
5. toast
6. lift
7. trick
8. row

B

1. tap
2. hop
3. skip
4. drop
5. smell
6. fan
7. fill
8. step

C

1. fill
2. help
3. weed
4. feel
5. steal
6. play
7. climb
8. weep

D

1. hope
2. ride
3. drive
4. race
5. like
6. hike
7. skate
8. make

Unit 49

A

1. the girl's book
2. the tree's leaf
3. the lady's dress
4. the cow's horn
5. the car's wheels
6. the man's pen

B

1. the rainbow's colours
2. the house's roof
3. the farmer's horse
4. the piano's legs
5. the team's captain
6. the dog's bone
7. the worker's helmet
8. the teacher's book

Unit 50 Revision

A

Double last letter + ing:

swim

chop

hop

plan

Drop e + ing:

chase

skate

hope

bake

B

1. dropping
2. skating
3. running
4. gazing
5. diving
6. slipping
7. biting
8. skipping

C

1. the book's pages
2. the pen's ink
3. the boy's jumper
4. the knife's blade
5. the worker's shovel
6. the farmer's tractor
7. the wasp's sting
8. the horse's bridle

Unit 51 Test

1. swimming
2. flapping
3. digging
4. mopping
5. dancing
6. waving
7. pasting
8. hoping
9. skipped
10. boy's
11. teacher's
12. book's

Unit 52

A

1. we've
2. it's
3. wasn't
4. can't
5. didn't
6. I'll
7. I'm
8. isn't

B

1. he is
2. does not
3. what is
4. they are
5. we have
6. he will
7. who is
8. she will

C

1. I've
2. can't
3. what's
4. doesn't

Unit 53

A

1. box
2. bank
3. sink
4. train
5. box
6. bank
7. sink
8. train

B

1. pen
2. post
3. match
4. ball
5. jam
6. bill
7. bark
8. crane

Unit 54

A

1. comb (b)
2. lamb (b)
3. thistle (t)
4. knee (k)
5. calf (l)
6. palm (l)
7. knife (k)
8. castle (t)

B

1. crumb
2. bomb
3. school
4. thistle
5. limb
6. scent
7. yolk
8. sword

Unit 55

A

1. bed
2. lake
3. cup
4. small
5. duck
6. ball
7. week
8. bread

B

1. ship
2. mouse
3. star
4. drum
5. sock
6. head
7. bird
8. block
9. chair

Unit 56

A

1. gorilla
2. gymnasium
3. garden
4. goat
5. gem
6. giant
7. grape
8. giraffe

B

1. comet
2. circle
3. coffee
4. city
5. cactus
6. circus
7. candle
8. fence

Unit 57

1. cricket
2. frozen
3. dream
4. blanket
5. grease
6. branch
7. claw
8. flower

B

1. slipper
2. prince
3. scone
4. snow
5. smoke
6. triangle
7. spanner
8. twenty

Unit 58

A

1. straw
2. scribble
3. strict
4. scratch
5. shrub
6. shrink
7. sprain
8. spring

B

1. straight
2. street
3. shrimp
4. sprint
5. scrub
6. shrine
7. scream
8. spread

Unit 59

1. bucket
2. fish
3. cheese
4. cricket
5. chick
6. peach
7. shovel
8. shampoo

B

1. throne
2. throat
3. squeak
4. squirt
5. three
6. square
7. squirrel

Unit 60

A

1. car / pet
2. rab / bit
3. ped / al
4. cam / el
5. pet / al
6. buck / et
7. pen / cil
8. shov / el

B

1. gravel
2. sandal
3. buckle
4. helmet
5. orbit
6. fragile
7. magnet
8. fossil

Unit 61 Revision

A

Silent k:
knife
knee

Silent b:
plumber
thumb

Silent t:
castle
thistle

Silent h:
school
hour

B

Hard g:
ground
guard
green
gate

Soft g:
genie
gypsy
ginger
giraffe

C

Hard c:
cousin
climb
camel
cabbage

Soft c:
city
cigar
cement
cell

Unit 62 Test 1

1. comb
2. thistle
3. strict
4. spread
5. giant
6. circus
7. cricket
8. slipper
9. cheese
10. squirt
11. bucket
12. helmet

Unit 63 Test 2

1. lamb
2. school
3. scribble
4. straw
5. giraffe
6. cactus
7. frozen
8. spanner
9. square
10. chick
11. pencil
12. shovel

Unit 64

A

1. colder
2. harder
3. shorter
4. sicker
5. warmer
6. faster
7. deeper
8. softer

B

1. taller
2. slower
3. neater
4. smaller
5. longer
6. sharper

Unit 65

A

1. invisible
2. explode
3. subway
4. postpone

B

1. submarine
2. bicycle
3. nonsmoking
4. mistake
5. untidy
6. triangle

Unit 66

A

1. brightly
2. enjoyable
3. collection
4. poisonous
5. expensive
6. careful
7. foolish
8. library

B

1. breathless
2. stylish
3. station
4. tiresome
5. dangerous
6. guitarist
7. attendant
8. edible

Unit 67

A

1. apron
2. chicken
3. fountain
4. turkey
5. daisy
6. tennis

B

1. broken
2. mountain
3. tractor
4. berry
5. trolley
6. luggage
7. dollar
8. mother

Unit 68 Revision

A

+ or:
doctor
actor
motor
tractor

+ er:
teacher
powder
rubber
scooter

+ ar:
dollar
collar
sugar
cellar

+ en:
children
kitten
garden
chicken

B

1. bicycle
2. triangle
3. octopus
4. submarine
5. explosion
6. forehead

Unit 69 Test

1. warmer
2. shorter
3. bicycle
4. triangle
5. useless
6. library
7. station
8. tennis
9. broken
10. mother
11. teacher
12. fountain

Unit 70

A

1. bus
2. tap
3. pram
4. ant
5. wolf
6. sail

7. seat
8. ring

B

1. pool
2. bowl
3. last
4. care
5. star
6. wasp
7. shoe
8. dew

Unit 71

A

1. ring
2. stop
3. liar
4. tide
5. tea
6. ape
7. rose
8. team

B

1. seat
2. star
3. plum
4. pear
5. vase
6. lamp
7. owl
8. rope

Unit 72

1. beard
2. mouse
3. home
4. feather
5. wolf
6. bark
7. fish
8. horse
9. money
10. puppy
11. pony
12. beach
13. pear
14. fairy
15. orange

Unit 73 Review

A

Long a:
snake
cake
Short a:
apple
splash
Long e:
teeth
here
Short e:
cent
wept
Long i:
spider
hive
Short i:
swift
finger
Long o:
woke
pony
Short o:
frog
stop

B

+ s:
eggs
houses
monkeys
trays
+ es:
buses
catches
boxes
bushes
Change y to i + es:
flies
lollies
stories
ponies

Unit 74 Test 1

1. whale
2. match
3. easy
4. picnic
5. catches
6. dresses
7. foxes
8. toys
9. donkeys
10. football
11. strawberries
12. armchair

Unit 75 Test 2

1. toe
2. clock
3. music
4. under
5. bark
6. purple
7. bottle
8. doctor
9. pinned
10. dragged
11. kicking
12. dropped

Unit 76 Test 3

1. wore
2. verse
3. heard
4. first
5. goose
6. soup
7. house
8. hoping
9. driving
10. chopping
11. swimming
12. knife